SNAFU FUBAR:

Nothing Heroic

BOB DIXON

Say what you want about our heroes, there's no arguing with their great taste in sticks. If you want to smoke the same cigars as Snafu and the General, here are where you can get these fine cigars.

Blanco Cigars
www.blancocigars.com
Córdoba & Morales Cigars
www.cnmcigars.com
Rolling Thunder Cigars
www.rtcigars.com
To follow Bob Dixon
www.facebook.com/dixonbob
Cover art- Jacob Miller
Cover layout and colors – Udo Wooten
Book design by Inkstain Interior Book Designing

ISBN: 1539002241
ISBN-13:978-1539002246

This book is dedicated to anyone who
enjoys the company of close friends,
cigars and good libations like my friends from
the Weekly Tradition and the Florida Cigar Club.

Igor

a real Man
can lit his
cigar anywhere

SNAFU FUBAR:

Nothing Heroic

PROLOGUE

Nothing Heroic

The story you are about to read is the true story of made-up comic book characters living in a small town that does not exist anywhere except within the confines of these pages. That being said, this desolate dot on the map is one of the top fifty vacation spots among made-up comic book cities.

For years, people believed that the world was flat. This same breed of people roam the earth today. They are the ones who believe in Bigfoot, aliens, paranormal activity, an honest politician or — even, dare we say it — people with superpowers who go around in costumes fighting the forces of evil. None of these creatures exist. As for the people who believe in them...they are fucking idiots.

That being said, the story you are about to read is a tale of two such costumed vigilantes and their perilous fight against the clutches of evil...well...that and their unending battle with alcoholism and other vices that are contrary to healthy living.

New York City has long been known as the Mecca for super-powered beings, both good and evil. Anyone who wants to make a name for themselves is here. Villain and hero alike both know the importance of making it big in New York City. Therefore, our story takes place far away, in the town of Lost Hope, Florida.

CHAPTER 1

Wank the One-Eyed Wonder Weasel

Snafu Fubar made his way across his kitchen, wearing nothing but his fluorescent orange boxer shorts. It was a sight no one needed to see. Those obnoxiously bright shorts were overlapped by a hairy stomach which had been carefully crafted by the consumption of entirely too much alcohol. Why, just last Christmas, Snafu received two thank you notes tucked into Christmas cards from guys who worked at a local brewery. They credited him with being solely responsible for their kids being able to attend Ivy League colleges.

It was one of Snafu's prouder moments. He thought about framing the letters and keeping them above the fireplace. But, since he didn't have the money to frame them or even a fireplace to hang them above, he chose to display them on the fridge, using magnets from the local strip club.

Bang! Bang! Bang! "Anyone home?"

Snafu looked at the wooden door, hoping whoever was on the other side would just go away.

Bang! Bang! Bang! They did not. "Are you home?" Snafu groaned and rolled his eyes, realizing that there was no way to avoid the truly disagreeable woman who was hammering on the door.

"Of course I'm home. Where else would I be at this un-godly hour?" Snafu snarled.

"It's almost 5 in the afternoon, you lousy bum! Open the damn door."

Snafu's shoulders sagged as he resigned himself to doing just that. There stood his neighbor, Sally. She was an un-pleasant woman who looked as if she had not only fallen out of the ugly tree and hit every branch on the way down, but also had experienced the misfortune of someone cutting the tree up into smaller pieces and beating her ass with it over and over. She weighed in at just over 4oo pounds and, without pride, Snafu had to admit that on more than one occasion, he had spent the night with her in compromising positions. He had videotaped some of their trysts to remind himself to quit drinking, however after seeing the videos, he usually became quite depressed and drank a hell of a lot more in order to forget about the occasion.

"What do you want?"

"I ran out of milk."

"Ever hear of a store?"

"I didn't come over here for any grief from you. Do you have any milk or not?"

Snafu hung his head in defeat and sauntered over to the fridge. He reached in and grabbed a half gallon of milk that was several weeks out of date, opened the cap, caught a whiff of the contents, and immediately replaced the lid. The milk smelled worse than he did after a week of binge drinking and sleeping in dumpsters. For a moment, it was all he could do not to blow chunks all over Sally...although that would certainly run her off for a while.

He held the milk jug out to her. "Yep. Got milk and it's only a few weeks out of date; take as much as you'd like."

Sally gingerly took the container and held it at arm's length. She could smell the milk through the carton. "What the hell? That's disgusting!"

"And having to look at you the first thing in the morning isn't?"

Sally thrust the milk back at Snafu. "Have you ever thought about suicide?"

"No, why?"

"You should."

"Look, do you want the milk or not?"

"Hell no, I don't want that disgusting shit!"

"Fine! I'll give it to Tripod!" Snafu bent over and began to pour some of the spoiled milk into a bowl.

Tripod made his way into the kitchen. He was a black cat with only three legs and, like his owner, always seemed to be sporting the homeless, neglected look. He glanced at the milk bowl, glared at Snafu and Sally, and promptly took a piss in the middle of the floor before stalking off in protest.

"Your cat just pissed on the floor!"

"Yeah, he does that when he gets mad."

"Why does your cat only have three legs?"

"Let's just say he'll never get drunk and play with the

garbage disposal in the middle of a lightning storm again."

Sally frowned at Snafu and just shook her head. "You give your cat beer?"

"Hell no!" Snafu sounded offended. "He prefers tequila. See?"

They both peered into the living room where Tripod sat on the couch, his two front paws wrapped around a tequila bottle that he was gingerly tipping into a small bowl on the TV tray. He slurped the tequila from the bowl then turned and glared at both of them, meowing twice rather loudly as if to say "fuck you". He then licked his own nuts, turned his back on them, farted twice and went back to sleep. Snafu grinned from ear to ear, beaming with pride. Sally was far from amused.

"My God, that's disgusting!" Sally fanned the smell away from her.

Snafu sniffed the air. "Oh yeah. He definitely had sardines last night, no doubt about it!" Snafu chuckled to himself as Sally turned green. "I'll tell you what...old Tripod there could knock a buzzard off a shit wagon!"

Without another word, Sally turned and marched out of the trailer in a huff, slamming the door behind her. Still grinning, Snafu looked down fondly at Tripod.

"Hell, if I had known that was all it took to get rid of her, I would have gladly done it myself." Snafu laughed as he opened a can of sardines and placed them on Tripod's TV tray. "Good boy, Tripod!" Tripod lifted a paw as if to give Snafu a high five, let one rip again and went back to sleep.

Snafu used speed dial to call his only friend. "Are we heading out on patrol tonight?"

"Yes. Let me think of a clever way to get out of the house and I'll meet you at the corner store. We need supplies." By supplies, his friend meant beer. Snafu closed his phone and stood in front of the refrigerator.

'The city is dirty and smelly. Ripe for the taking,' thought Snafu. He held his arm up, took a whiff of his armpit, and let out a loud exclamation. "Whew! That's a strong bond I share with my fair city!"

Snafu grabbed a beer and took a quick shower. He considered putting on the bright pink Speedos with the little cape attached and the cut-off T-shirt that showed his stomach, but decided to go with the neon orange jogging pants and camo T-shirt instead. Snafu grabbed the cooler with wheels and headed outside, locking the door to his trailer as he left. Tripod took another sip of tequila before using the remote to order pay-per-view porn, thinking to himself that quality pussy was so hard to find these days.

General Nuisance fumbled with his keys, trying to unlock the door to his house while coming up with a good excuse for going back out tonight. The man known around his neighborhood as 'the creepy guy who hung out in front of his workshop with the other creepy guy drinking beer, smoking cigars, and talking about sex all night' entered his home.

"Oh, wow honey. I didn't know you were home tonight. I thought you had a 'girl's night out' or something."

General Nuisance's wife looked startled. The sound of keys in the front door had brought her into the living room at a run, wearing nothing but a half-open house coat. "Oh, it got canceled. I thought you were going to be gone tonight."

"Well I was considering going out to sleep with another woman if you didn't mind." General Nuisance silently cursed himself as, once again, he hadn't really thought out a good escape plan.

General Nuisance's wife just rolled her eyes. "Fine. Just be sure to pick up a loaf of bread, some milk and my tampons while you're out. Oh yeah...and a candy bar."

When General Nuisance made his way into the bedroom to change, he immediately noticed a naked person slumped in his bed, drinking a beer. That individual looked remarkably like his neighbor, Jim.

"I can explain," mumbled the bearded man, who was by now frantically trying to untangle himself from the sheets and spilling his beer all over the bed in the process.

General Nuisance stormed back into the living room where his wife still stood looking down at the floor. She hadn't even bothered to close her house coat. "What exactly is going on here?" he demanded.

"Ah, well...it's...well —"

"Yeah. Exactly as I thought. You're afraid I'm really going out to sleep with another woman, so you invited one of your girlfriends over for a threesome, hoping it will make me shirk my sworn duty...and as much as I appreciate you inviting your rather ugly, bearded girlfriend over, I have things I really need to do tonight so you will have to put your kinkiness on hold. Maybe if your friend is still here when I get home and I'm really drunk...and I mean really, really drunk...we can see about pursuing that avenue, but our city needs me to protect it tonight even more than you need big daddy's loving." General Nuisance gave his wife a kiss on her forehead. "On a different note, Hun...although I really like the idea of having sex with two women at the same time, is there any chance you can get a better looking one than this one? I mean, she is kinda fat and ugly...not to mention her titties are strange looking and sagging...plus there is all that facial hair." General Nuisance's wife stared at her husband and pondered for a moment whether he really was that stupid or if he was toying with her. Satisfied that he truly was a moron, she sauntered back to the bedroom shaking her head.

'Where are you running off to?" Jim was still completely naked and already half way out the window. Jim turned to speak, balancing precariously on the windowsill so as to not fall. This left his hairy, naked ass waggling in the air for all of the neighbors to see. The kids next door playing football probably didn't appreciate the view.

"Your husband is home. I'm getting out of here!"

She laughed. "He's getting dressed to go play superhero with his heterosexual life mate. We should have most of the night, so get back in here, close the window and come back to bed. It's cold in here and I need some warming up." Jim backed his ass through the window and promptly fell on the grimy, nasty carpet, barely missing landing on the heel of a fuzzy pink stiletto.

●

Meanwhile, across the street from the trailer park, in a convenience store that General Nuisance and Snafu Fubar frequented, a robber had just entered, brandishing a pistol.He pointed it at the clerk behind the counter, a young boy who had not yet reached legal drinking age and who still had a zit party in full swing on his chubby face. "Put your hands in the air and give me the money!" The clerk looked confused for a moment and then shrugged.

"I can't do both."

"Huh...what?"

The clerk rolled his eyes. "I can't put my hands in the air and give you the money."

"Fine. Put one hand in the air and hand me the money with the other one." The robber gestured with the gun.

"OK, which hand?"

"Right...no, wait a minute. Left."

"Left hand up or left hand get the money?"

The robber banged his head against the counter three times and glared at the clerk. "Left hand get the money."

Ding Ding.

The robber and clerk both looked toward the store's door, through which a female customer had just entered. She was blond, with a great body and nice rack, but her face was ugly as sin. "Can I get twenty on pump five?"

The robber stepped towards her, motioning with the gun. "Lie down on the floor now!"

"What? Really? Have you seen this floor? I'd probably have a higher chance of survival if you just shoot me. I think I'll take my chances!"

The robber glanced down at the floor. "OK. Point taken. Just sit on the floor."

"Really wish I hadn't picked today to wear stilettos and this damn mini skirt with no panties," griped the customer. "I mean, if I'm going to catch an STD, I really wanted to do it the fun way." She looked about as graceful as a giraffe on roller skates as she tried several maneuvers to get down on the floor without giving the clerk and the robber their own private peep show.

General Nuisance met Snafu in the parking lot of the convenience store. They did the handshake, the fist bump, the high five, the gang sign, the chest bump and the butt slap — to which they both said in unison, "NO GO HOMO!" This, of course, made it perfectly acceptable for two grown men to slap each other on the ass.

"Do you see what I see?" General Nuisance pointed into the convenience store that held his beloved beer.

"Yeah, some idiot sitting on a disease ridden floor.Hope she knows there are more enjoyable ways to catch an STD."

"I agree, but I wasn't talking about her. Look again…a robber!"

"Cool! You wanna hand out some Bronze Age justice?"

General Nuisance poked his friend in the arm. "I got one better…Iron Age justice, huh, huh?"

"Oh, that's just stupid! What did the Iron Age have that the Bronze Age didn't?"

"Really? Asia was smelting tin and brass by then…you can't top that. What was your Bronze Age doing? Cave men were still circle jerking on dinosaurs' corpses."

"That's the Stone Age, you idiot." Snafu shook his head.

"You can be so dumb at times."

While Snafu Fubar and General Nuisance debated over the kind of justice they were going to hand out, things inside the store took a bizarre turn.

"Man, my drawer is gonna be off. I'm gonna have to over-charge all my customers tonight," the clerk whined as he looked down at his till.

"Shut up! Just get the money," screamed the robber.

"I don't feel so well," said the female customer, whose face was now a sickly shade of green. She burped once then farted. A moment later, she puked all over the floor and shit herself.

"Crap! Now I'm going to have to mop the floor and man, I was really hoping to leave that for the morning shift. I mean I could kind of push everything under the candy counter. There's a good chance no one would notice and I could just place a wet floor sign where she is at. Yeah...the more I think about it, I'm pretty sure that would work."

"Oh my God! Why are you taking so long?" The robber pointed the gun at the clerk again.

The store's door swung open. Loud rock music blared as Snafu and General Nuisance entered the store. "I'm here to kick some ass and hand out -", Snafu sighed, "Industrial Revolution era justice!"

"See?!? Was that so hard?" General Nuisance asked with a smile.

The robber grabbed the clerk by his shirt collar. "This is why you should have moved faster. Both of you get down on the ground now...or the clerk dies."

General Nuisance and Snafu both looked down at the female customer who was now shaking and in the midst of some kind of convulsion. "Yeah, that's just not going to happen," Snafu said.

"Son, put the gun down." General Nuisance spoke as calmly as a man being threatened with sitting on a disease-ridden floor could speak.

"How about I shoot you?!" screamed the frustrated robber as he pointed the gun first at General Nuisance then at Snafu.

"Yeah, shoot those costumed freaks!" chimed in the clerk.

"You stay out of this!" the robber yelled at the clerk.

"Why are you rooting for the robber?" asked Snafu.

"I don't know...just seemed like we were connecting...I

don't get a lot of social interaction here."

The robber looked back and forth between the costumed vigilantes and the clerk. "Shit! I don't know who to shoot first!"

"Please God, let it be me! *Bleck!*" said the customer on the floor as she puked again.

"Well, while you decide that, I'm going to grab a Slushee," Snafu said as he strolled toward the back of the store.

"Yeah. Me too. Let's grab the beer and some beef jerky while we're at it," General Nuisance said as he patted the robber on the shoulder and walked past him.

The robber snatched the money from the clerk's hand and ran out of the store. "Ya'll are fuckin' crazy!"

The clerk, looking as though he'd just lost his best friend or a beloved pet, leaned over the edge of the counter.

"Call me...I mean if you want to hang out or something," the clerk yelled as the robber made his escape. When he didn't get a response, the clerk slumped back against his stool.

"They never call."

CHAPTER 2
Cuddle the Kielbasa

The contractor looked over the blueprints, took a sip from his coffee and then gave them a once over again. He always preferred when the blue prints made perfect sense to him...most contractors did. But there were things in this plan he just wasn't so sure about.

"Hey, Mr. Overlord, got some questions on yer machine here." His New York accent was coming through more than his client cared for...yet another reminder that he could not cut it in the Big Apple as a supervillain.

"That's 'The Evil Overlord'."

"Huh?"

"You referred to me as 'Mr. Overlord' which is incorrect. I'm 'The Evil Overlord' and although your small excuse for a mind may not be able to comprehend the importance of name recognition, believe me when I tell you that it is very important to me.

"Yeah, OK, got ya. Anyways, I was looking over your design for your 'rec room'. So ya got this room that's got moving walls and spikes and trap doors that dead ferrets fall out of."

"Yes." The Evil Overlord couldn't help but to smile as he thought about the dead ferrets falling down on some unsuspecting superhero.

"Well...just seems very ineffectual if you're gonna torture a superhero. "

"Uh...um hmm...no one is torturing anyone. Does this look like Gitmo?" The Evil Overlord looked around the room quickly, hoping to locate a weapon that could be used to silence the contractor.

The contractor gave The Evil Overlord a big fake wink. "Gotcha, but if you 'were' gonna torture a superhero, he could escape like ten different ways."

"Well I seriously doubt there are that many ways to escape."

"Oh sure...I mean look here," the contractor said, moving to stand by him and turning the blueprints so The Evil Overlord could see them correctly. "Ya got this air vent thingy going on here, plus the whole underground river with the alligators. Though, granted they have to get by the gators, which is a nice touch."

"Thank you." The Evil Overlord began to smile with pride at the appreciation for his dastardly plan.

"But still plausible for a superhero, especially if he is like 'Gatorman' or something like that and can control gators." The Evil Overlord stopped smiling and narrowed his eyes to little more than slits.

"Well that's very true but that's only two ways; that's hardly ten."

"Well, then you have this shabby lock you plan on putting on the cell door. I mean...granted you save a few bucks, but in the end shoddy materials makes for shoddy craftsmanship."

The Evil Overlord looked around the room again, hoping to find a hammer but did not see anything close enough to grab. "OK, 'Mr. Hotshot Torture Design Specialist'." The Evil Overlord said this while making quotation marks in the air. He loved air quotation marks. "How would you do it?"

"Who me? Oh I'm not an evil mastermind."

"Yeah, that's what I thought," grinned The Evil Overlord. "Typical isn't it? Criticize other people's dreams but have no plan of your own."

"I'd drown them in shit."

"Oh good lord! Are you fucking serious?" The Evil Overlord rolled his eyes and shook his head.

The contractor's eyes darkened as his face took on a crazed look. "Yeah, I'm DEAD serious. Drown them in a shitty pond, just like I had to do with dear old Mommy, because sometimes little boys don't like to ride ponies, and no one should ever be made to ride a pony, especially one that kicks and bites and is named Ralph Waldo and makes all the other kids laugh and point. But that's OK. I tracked those kids down when I was done with Mommy, oh yes I did. If mommy would have just listened...but would she? Nooooo, mommy wouldn't listen...she never listened to me...always pushing...but I showed her...oh, hell yes I did."

The Evil Overlord took a few steps back. "Ah...yeah."

'Talk about the things they don't mention on Bubba's List,' he thought to himself. "Hey, ah look...ah...listen here. You seem to have some stuff going on...like some kind of emotional trauma type stuff. How about taking the afternoon off...get your head back in the game... maybe come back and try again on Monday?"

"Are you sure? Because I'm telling you, I can design you one kick-ass torture room."

The Evil Overlord guided the contractor to the front door by the elbow. "I have total faith in you. You go home and design it and give me a call when it's done and I'll get back to you."

Da Bad Guy entered as the contractor exited the house. "Is he done already or is he going for supplies?"Da Bad Guy put the groceries on the counter and started to unpack them.

"Oh, he's done alright. He mentioned some serious issues about his mother and a pony. He wanted to build a shit pond to drown our enemies in. Apparently he may have drowned his mother in one...not sure about the pony."

"What the hell...are you serious? Do you have any clue how much shit it would take to keep that filled?!"Da Bad Guy started to reach for a chocolate pudding cup that was sitting on the counter, then quickly changed his mind when he realized what it looked like.

"I can't make stuff like this up." The Evil Overlord reached for the pudding cup that Da Bad Guy had just set back down. If Da Bad Guy didn't want it, then that meant more for him.

"Did he drown the pony as well?"

"Told you I didn't know, but I assume not since he didn't specifically mention it."

"Where the hell did you find that psycho?" Da Bad Guy felt his stomach turn as he watched The Evil Overlord eating the chocolate pudding and enjoying it a little too much. He realized then that he'd never be able to eat, or even look at, chocolate pudding again.

"Bubba's List, under the section for supervillains for hire. His ad was very nice...good references...thought he could help build our torture chamber." The Evil Overlord started putting the groceries away." I mean, we've hired henchmen from there before and always have had good results."

"Did his ad mention anything about being unstable and

having mommy issues?"

"No...not really. Well...now that you mention it, there was a small cartoon with the ad that struck me as a little odd at the time." The Evil Overlord looked down at the ground a bit sheepishly.

Da Bad Guy leaned over the bar. "What kind of cartoon?"

"There was a guy hitting a woman with a tire iron and yelling BITCH! Seemed weird at the time, but figured it was kinda folksy...you know, kitschy."

"That's what you call a big fucking hint!" yelled Da Bad Guy.

"In hind sight I can see that now, but at the time it seemed like a good idea."

"How about now?"

"Well, I'm certainly second guessing it just a little bit."

"I would hope so!" Da Bad Guy patted The Evil Overlord on the back. "Next time I'll go through the ads with you and we will make a choice that is a little better fit for our needs, OK?"

"I appreciate that." The Evil Overlord looked through his telescope. "Let's see what our mortal enemies are up to to-night."

•

General Nuisance and Snafu Fubar sat on the deck of the workshop that they had appropriately named 'The Fucking Nuisance Cave' in a pair of lawn chairs with a large cooler between them. In one hand, they both had a Blanco Nine cigar, in the other, an ice cold beer.

"Man, I'm telling you, she did not want me going on patrol tonight. She went so far as to bring over one of her girl-friends for a threesome."

"Bullshit!" Snafu took a drag from his cigar. "No way your wife invited some chick over so you guys could do a three-some."

"I'm telling you, she did."

"Was she cute?"

"Well I ain't saying all of that now," laughed the General. "If I'm being honest with you, she was pretty homely look-ing."

"Well, ugly women need love too, you know." Snafu laughed as he took a sip from his beer.

"You'll get no arguments from me there," said General Nuisance. "But this chick has some of the saddest titties I've ever seen...plus she had way too much facial hair."

"Wouldn't it be cool if tits came with a squeaky toy inside of them? I mean, can you imagine how awesome that would be? I mean, you think they are fun to play with now; imagine if they squeaked when you squeezed them."General Nuisance was in mid-swallow of his beer and thought for sure he was about to choke.

General Nuisance gave Snafu the 'what the hell is wrong with you' look, then wiped the beer from his chin with the back of his hand.

"Could you imagine how loud a strip club would be if tits had a squeaky toy in them?" Snafu grinned like he had just won the lottery.

"Dude, I mention titties and you just go off on an irrele-vant tangent! What are you? Twelve?"

"No, thirteen," laughed Snafu. "But seriously, you're try-ing to tell me you wouldn't like playing with boobies that squeaked when you squeezed them?"

General Nuisance's face lit up with a small grin. "OK, you got me on that one. I mean, who wouldn't?"

"Yeah...that's what I thought." They both tipped their beers as if making a toast to their obvious genius and chugged to see who would finish first. Snafu, of course, was triumphant.

•

Meanwhile, The Evil Overlord and Da Bad Guy were each enjoying a glass of Merlot while monitoring the activities across the street and planning their takeover of the city.

"There they sit, plotting ways to stop my diabolical plans." The Evil Overlord stepped back from his telescope, rubbing his hands together in the way that villains do.

"They look like they are just drinking beer and talking about titties," said Da Bad Guy as he positioned himself behind the telescope and turned it slightly so that he could see into General Nuisance's bedroom. "Man that sure is an ugly chick with some sad tits his wife is having sex with. Kinda looks like their neighbor."

"You are such a simpleton that your mind cannot comprehend the genius that we are challenged by, or how truly dangerous our opponents are. As we sit here and plan the takeover of this fair city, I can promise you that they are over there desperately trying to figure out a way to stop our plans."

"Look, evil overlord –"

"That's 'The Evil Overlord'!"

Da Bad Guy sighed. "Do you really think adding 'The' before your name really makes you sound that much more important and fierce? Seriously, don't you think it's kind of stupid?"

The Evil Overlord got a sad look on his face as his lower lip started to quiver and his eyes misted up.

"Ugh...OK fine. THE Evil Overlord. I'm not even sure these two guys know we are alive."

The Evil Overlord smiled and wiped his eyes. "Ha! I laugh at your ignorance. How do they not know of The Evil Overlord and his side kick, Da Bad Guy?! No. Do not let the good General and his sloppy looking companion fool you, for they are more witty than they appear...so much so that the secret location of their hideout, The Fucking Nuisance Cave, has long been kept from me."

"First off, I'm no one's sidekick. If anything, you're mine. Secondly, I'm pretty sure that the porch where they drink at every night that has the cardboard sign they put up that reads 'The Fucking Nuisance Cave' is the location of their hideout...but I could be wrong." Da Bad Guy took a sip of his Arbor Mist Blackberry Merlot, happy that he'd remembered to pick up a few bottles while at the grocery store.

The Evil Overlord contemplated this for a moment. "No, no...I must disagree with you. That is strictly a ruse to distract anyone who might be spying on them as they keep the real whereabouts of the cave a secret, knowing full well that if it and their secret identities ever fell into my evil clutches, they would be doomed."

"I guess you're right. I mean after all, what kind of heroes would they be if they just sat on the front porch drinking beer, smoking cigars, and talking about tits all night," agreed Da Bad Guy.

They both slumped down in their chairs, sipped their wine, and pondered that very question.

CHAPTER 3
Jerkin' the Gherkin'

Snafu took a sip of his beer. "I'm telling you, dude, that little cashier down at the Quick Split has some really nice knockers."

"I'm not saying they aren't nice. I just don't like the super huge ones as far as to play with. I mean, they're fun to look at and all but you know more than a mouth full is a waste. Besides...most knockers like that are fake," laughed General Nuisance.

"Well, it's not like fake tits taste funny or anything," replied Snafu.

"Not saying they do. I just don't like the feel of them. I prefer the more natural feeling of a woman's breast. Fake ones usually feel hard. I kind of like the squishy feel of a natural breast."

"Well if that's the case, then why aren't you in your bedroom right now with your wife and Ms. Saggy Titties? I'm pretty sure those are natural but I can't imagine I'd like the way they would feel in my hands."

General Nuisance started to respond when he noticed a man walking up to The Fucking Nuisance Cave.

"Excuse me, gentlemen. Mind if I have a moment of your time?"

"Whatever you're selling, we're not buying." General Nuisance took another puff of his cigar.

"Unless of course you're selling shots. I mean I could use a shot to go with this beer," said Snafu.

"Yeah, if you're selling shots we'll take a few rounds," agreed General Nuisance. "Naturally that goes without saying."

"I'm not selling anything," answered the man who was becoming somewhat annoyed. "And why the hell would I be going door to door selling shots? That's just ridiculous. I mean, who the hell does that?"

"Well, granted you would make more money if you were a hot chick," answered Snafu. "I mean let's face it, men prefer women bartenders to male ones."

"I don't know about that...I mean if you're bringing me alcohol, I'm pretty happy no matter who you are," replied General Nuisance. "Speaking of which, I'm out and it's your turn to get them."

"Yeah, me too." Snafu got up and walked over to the cooler, made sure his ass was aimed at General Nuisance and the visitor, then leaned over, exposing about six inches of hairy, farting ass crack as he retrieved the beers.

"So did you enjoy that view you just had of my ass? Or would you have preferred to be looking at a sexy little beach bunny with nice knockers?" Snafu asked as he handed his friend a cold beer.

"I think I just tasted my own vomit," said the visitor.

"Consider yourself fortunate. I'm considering gouging out my eyes in hopes that I can make sure that image isn't forever burned into my retina," General Nuisance said as he took a swig of his beer.

"I think that proves my point about male and female bartenders though."

"No, the only thing that proves is nobody wants to see your fat, hairy, naked ass bending over a beer cooler," snorted General Nuisance.

"Look guys...I'm not selling door to door shots. My name is Peter. I'm from the home owners association. There have been complaints about some of the nightly activities going on at this residence and I am here to issue a formal warning to you."

"Like what?" General Nuisance asked as Snafu and he exchanged glances.

"The neighbors say that you two sit out here til all hours of the night drinking beer, smoking cigars, and talking about getting laid and that kind of behavior is simply not going to be tolerated in such a fine upstanding neighborhood such as ours!"

"Well, I would hope not...that's disgusting! There is no way we would just sit out here doing that. I'll have you know that we are superheroes on patrol, looking after the safety and security of this fine city of ours," General Nuisance exclaimed defiantly.

"Oh, give me a break!" said Peter. "I've watched you guys for the last week and all you do is drink, smoke those nasty cigars and talk about sex. It's disgusting!"

"Well to laymen such as yourself, it might look like that. But rest assured we are forever vigilant in patrolling the city to assure that the forces of evil are not triumphant." Snafu took a puff of his cigar and he and General Nuisance clinked their beer bottles together in a mock toast.

"Then maybe I should hang out -"

"You mean patrol." Snafu interrupted.

"OK then, maybe I should patrol with you a few nights and see if you can change my opinion of your nightly activities."

General Nuisance and Snafu exchanged a nervous glance. "I'm not sure that would be possible."

"Why not?"

"Well, to be on patrol with us, you would have to be a superhero like us," answered General Nuisance, "which you obviously are not."

"Fine! I'm a superhero, so I can patrol with you," snapped Peter.

"You can't just say you're a superhero and expect us to

believe it. You have to have powers and a costume...shit like that. Go throw yourself in a nuclear reactor and come back when you're glowing green and we can discuss it." Snafu took another sip of his beer.

"And don't forget a cool costume," added General Nuisance. "We would hate for you to tarnish our good image."

"Fine...I'll be back in a few minutes." Peter said as he stormed off.

"Can you believe that mother fucker? Accusing us of just hanging out when here we are, putting life and limb on the line to make sure that the city is safe?! Some people have such nerve!"

"I feel ya, bro," answered General Nuisance. "I'm not sure if I have ever been more insulted in my entire life."

"I'm pretty sure I have. I mean, face it. Look at me...I'm sure people talk bad about me when I'm not around," replied Snafu.

"They do it when you're around too...usually you're just too busy talking to notice."

"Really?"

"Yeah, sorry to be the one to have to tell ya."

Snafu held his beer up for a toast. "I appreciate it, man.

I mean after all, that is what friends are for."

General Nuisance got up and went into the workshop to relieve himself. Normally he and Snafu just did it on the side of The Fucking Nuisance Cave, but since he had to retrieve a second round of cigars, he thought he would be civilized.

"Hey Snafu! Come here...we're on TV again." General Nuisance yelled as he unmuted the TV.

"Awesome!" Snafu replied as he entered The Fucking Nuisance Cave and gave General Nuisance a fist bump.

On the screen was a female reporter. She was standing with the clerk from the local convenience store."It seems like some ill-conceived attempt to play superhero happened here tonight."

The TV screen cut to a split window as the anchorman broke in. "I'm sorry Julie, did you say superheroes?"

"Yes, sadly James, superheroes.Some moronic attempt at vigilante justice...very sad." Julie shook her head from side to side as she spoke. "I'm standing here with the clerk who was robbed at gunpoint. Sir, could you tell us what happened here tonight?"

"I was robbed! Well, the place was robbed. I mean, he didn't take my wallet or anything. For that matter, he didn't take anyone's…would have thought that would have been a good thing for him as a robber to do." said the clerk."My boss, Mr. Sanjay, is gonna be pissed!"

"That's awful, you brave soul." Julie did her best to sound like the sympathetic reporter.

"He was a beast of a man.Broad shoulders.Looked like he worked out a lot.Arms like tree branches…but you know…they'd probably feel good around you, make you feel really safe…really sexy…wanted…needed…" The clerk began to smile wistfully and stared off into nothing, having a private moment.

Julie's eyes lit up a little. "Hopefully I can get a sneak peek at him on the surveillance video soon."

"I don't remember him being all that great looking," Snafu said as he took a sip of beer.

"Don't hate," General Nuisance replied. "I mean, let's face it, he was a man among men."

"What the fuck dude, is he like your new man crush?"

"Fuck you! I'm just saying he was a good looking guy." General Nuisance shook his head. "Not like I'm trying to have sex with him or anything. Sheesh, just shut up and watch the fucking broadcast!"

"I bet he owned a golden retriever...and was good with kids.Probably knew how to sail, too...I hope he calls..." the clerk continued.

"As for our lame ass 'superheroes', did they say or do anything?" interrupted Julie.

"Something about industrial revolution justice." The clerk shook his head.

"Not bronze era justice? That would make more sense," questioned Julie.

"Dammit! See I told you bronze era justice was a better way to go!" Snafu shouted.

"Nah, it's all about industrial age revolution justice," General Nuisance replied. "They just don't see it yet. We are before our time. You have to trust me on this. I'm as right about this as I was those Enron stocks...just give it time."

Julie answered a question asked by the anchorman. "No, sadly James, it seems they said industrial revolution justice. It's clearly a mix up made by men with extremely small penises who are trying to compensate."

"What the fuck?" General Nuisance screamed at the TV.

"Yeah, that's just a little uncalled for," added Snafu.

"Julie, Julie, who's that woman being brought out on a

gurney? Me-ow!" Anchorman James sat up straighter and leered into the camera.

Julie turned to glance at the gurney that was taking the blond female customer out of the store. "Oh, just some slutty party girl that old men use as a sperm catcher. No one important."

"I'm sick, not deaf, you fucking whore! I can totally hear you!" the girl screamed as she was wheeled past the camera.

"Sorry," said Julie indignantly. "Was anything that I just said inaccurate?"

"No." the girl on the gurney closed her eyes and started to cry. "It's true, I am a slut...it's just that...my dad watches this channel." The girl on the gurney began to sob uncontrollably. Julie, unsure of what to do, patted the girl on the shoulder with her finger tip, not really wanting to touch her.

"Fine," Julie said shaking her head in frustration.She then looked directly at the camera, frowning."If you're the father of little sperm sponge here, she is a nice girl who never does anything wrong. If you're not her father...well...we have her contact information. She sat on the floor of this store without panties on, which means there is very little she will not do."

"Thank you," the girl said, wiping her tears from her cheeks. "Thank you for tellin' my daddy I'm a good girl!" The girl looked up and smiled at Julie.

"Wanna hear more about the robber?I have a pretty long diary entry about him and a few of his hairs that fell on the floor," interrupted the clerk.

"I think we're done," Julie said as she lowered her mike.

"Thankfully Julie didn't drop the ball and got party girl's info. For a moment I thought we were going to have to cruise the local hospitals looking for her," said the anchorman.

"You're a fucking jackass, Jim!" Julie was heard saying before the station switched back to the studio, cutting her off the air.

Turning back to the primary camera in the studio, James put on a big, white, fake Hollywood smile and looked as if he'd just won an Emmy. "Be sure to tune in tomorrow night viewers, when Julie will do a little underwater diving in the town's shitty ass water treatment plant. It's a little surprise we have been planning for her for quite some time."

"Wow, that was unfair...and they're the 'news leader'?" General Nuisance cut off the TV.

"No shit!" said Snafu. "I mean you filled out that online

survey. They even sent you a t-shirt."

"That's right, that shirt totally rocked. Wait, they trashed us! I'm burning that shirt," snapped General Nuisance. "I refuse to support any news agency that doesn't see the brilliance of what we do."

"Hey, maybe we can recruit that news chick...make her our sidekick."

"Nah, the last woman that came in here yakked on the floor, said something about a vague 'smell' and then ran like hell," replied General Nuisance. "Remember?"

"Oh yeah...how is Betty?"

"Well the rash is gone, I think, and I'm pretty sure she has stopped bathing in bleach. She still has the night terrors, but from what I understand, they seem to think that the group therapy is working."

"Well, that's good to hear," replied Snafu. "Guess you're right...I mean, let's face it...we are just not cut out to have a female side kick."

"Don't give up so soon, my friend. I mean, after swimming underwater in the town's shit and urine, this place will smell like roses!"

Snafu sniffed himself and then the room. "Roses. Really?"

General Nuisance took a deep sniff. "OK...maybe not exactly roses. Maybe more like wet dog. Same difference though."

"I'm back!" a voice called from outside of The Fucking Nuisance Cave.

"Peter is that...ah...you?" General Nuisance asked as he and Snafu took their seats. Both gaped at Peter who was now dressed up in some sort of brightly colored outfit.

"No...I'm The Flaming Unicorn! A new hero who just arrived in town to assist you as you patrol this fine city of ours," answered Peter.

"Peter, we're not going to let you join us just because you went home and dressed up in a lame ass outfit!" replied Snafu. "Hell, half of the clothes look like they belong to a cheap hooker anyways."

"Who is this Peter you speak of? I'm The Flaming Unicorn." Peter looked around nervously. "Ah, I don't know this Peter you speak of."

Snafu leaned a little closer so he could inspect something strapped to the top of Peter's head. "'Dude, is that a fucking dildo on your head?!"

"Ah no...ah...it's a horn." Peter replied.

"But it's made out of plastic," General Nuisance said as he and Snafu got up to take a closer look at Peter's costume.

"And it doesn't have a point on it." General Nuisance and Snafu both reached out to touch it.

"My mother won't let me play with sharp objects," protested Peter, backing away from the two men.

"But she'll let you play with her vibrator? What are you going to do, fuck the bad guys into submission with your dildo of death?" laughed Snafu.

"Dude...that's just seriously fucking disturbing," added General Nuisance as he and Snafu sat back down, simultaneously popping another beer. General Nuisance reached down and adjusted his crotch, checking to see if he had as much as what Peter had strapped to his head. Feeling satisfied, he took another sip of his beer.

"I'll prove I'm a superhero."

"And just how are you going to do that?"

"Look...there's a gang about to break into that car. I'll stop them! That should prove I'm legit," Peter yelled as he ran off.

Snafu and General Nuisance watched as Peter approached the three thugs breaking into a late model sedan. "Stop your villainous ways, for The Flaming Unicorn is here to impale you with justice!" Snafu and the General couldn't stop themselves from laughing.

"Think we should go help?" asked Snafu as he watched the thugs pound poor Peter into the ground.

"Nope. The boy has to learn to stand on his own two feet if he wants to be a superhero."

"Very true."

"Oh no!" Peter cried. "You broke off my magical horn!" screamed Peter as a vibrating sound became audible.

"Wow," chuckled Snafu. "That horn went right though the pants. That's the problem with having your costume made out of cheap fabric. Doesn't put up any resistance whatsoever in crucial times such as these," winced Snafu.

"Well, thankfully it didn't have a point on it," said General Nuisance as he looked away.

"Well, that and it found a natural cavity to go up," added Snafu. "Think we should go after them?"

"Hell no," answered General Nuisance as he took a puff of his cigar. "I mean hell...they are armed with the dildo of death and apparently are not afraid to use it."

"Well, you do have a point there."

"Which unfortunately Peter just got," laughed General Nuisance.

CHAPTER 4

Lubricating the Love Monkey

Snafu and General Nuisance looked longingly into the empty beer cooler, hoping against all hope that more beer would magically appear but, sadly, it was not to be. Teary eyed, they gave each other the drunken guy handshake that involves getting pulled into a half hug, to which both said "no go homo" — an important ritual to establish that they were not gay — and started to go their separate ways.

"Sure you don't want to crash on the couch?"

Snafu thought for a brief second. "Man, you've got that

ugly woman in there waiting for your threesome. I'd hate to interfere with the chance of that happening. Besides...after she is done with you, she might come out and jump me in my sleep if she were to see this much macho man meat asleep on your couch. Women can't get enough of me." Snafu let out a belch, scratched his ass and reached down to adjust his crotch.

"When you're right, you're right," General Nuisance said, shaking his head from side to side as he turned and entered the house, praying to all that was holy that his wife and her ugly girlfriend had passed out and that he would be able to get some rest.

Snafu stopped off at the convenience store on the way home and used his last three dollars to buy a can of beer and a lotto ticket. To his surprise, he won thirty dollars on the scratch off. With his winnings, he bought a twelve pack of beer and left the store, deciding to drop the extra twenty dollars into the night deposit at his bank, which was right on his way home.

"Love free beer money," Snafu mumbled as he shoved the money into the bank envelope. On the front of the envelope where the account information belonged, Snafu simply wrote 'Please deposit into my account', peeled one of the labels from a bottle of beer and stuck it to the envelope to cover postage, then dropped it into the night slot. "Well, that's that!" Snafu said with a grin.

As Snafu turned, he saw a man standing behind him. The man was holding his hand out in front of him, as if it were a gun, his thumb in the air and his index finger pointed at Snafu. The would-be robber didn't realize the mistake he was about to make. Not just the mistake of robbing a super-hero — the mistake of robbing Snafu Fubar.

Snafu took another sip of beer. "How can I help you?"

"Hi, my name is John and I'll be your robber for the evening." Snafu looked at the man, who looked a lot like the man who had tried to rob the convenience store earlier.

"But I don't need a robber."

"Doesn't matter if you need one or not," replied John. "I mean, it's kind of like insurance. You don't actually need it, but it is required."

"What kind of robber are you? I mean, you don't even have a gun. You're holding me up with your finger!"

"It's not a finger; it's a gun."

"Is not."

"Is too."

"Is not."

"Is too."

Snafu popped the top on another beer. "Not even I'm stupid enough to fall for that one, and believe me when I tell you, that's saying something."

John looked around for a brief moment, as if thinking. "It's a mime gun".

"But you're not a mime."

"How do you know?"

"Because you're fucking talking and mimes don't fucking talk."

Again John looked perplexed. "Maybe I used to be a mime."

Snafu stepped back cautiously. "What do you mean maybe? Either you were or you weren't. So which is it?"

"I was a mime...yeah that's it...absolutely! I was a dangerous mime too."

"Well, in that case, I'd better cooperate," Snafu replied. He threw both hands high in the air, forgetting the bottle of beer he was holding, dumping it's contents on his head. At that point, he started to cry.

"Quit crying."

"But I spilled my beersy weersy!"

"What are you, a baby?"

"No," sniffed Snafu. "Just hate to waste beer...it hurts my soul."

"Enough of this nonsense," yelled John. "Give me your cash and credit cards!"

"Sorry...can't do that. I just dropped my cash in the night deposit. Oh shit! I forgot to hold out beer money!" Snafu started getting teary again.

"But you have almost half a case right there by your feet!"

"As if that is going to survive the night," Snafu said rather proudly.

"Look, just shut up for a minute," John screamed, pointing his finger gun in Snafu's face. "Are you seriously telling me you don't have any cash?"

"None whatsoever."

"Fine, just give me your credit cards."

Snafu scratched his ass and farted. "No can do...don't have any."

"What the hell? Everyone has credit cards. It's the

American way!" John was pacing by this time.

Snafu sat down and tried to open a beer bottle with his feet while keeping his hands in the air. To John's surprise, Snafu was not only able to accomplish this seemingly impossible task, but was also able to drink a few sips from the bottle by holding it with his toes. "Would you trust me with a credit card?"

"Damn good point."

"I have a debit card I could give ya, but it doesn't work."

"What do you mean it 'doesn't work'?"

Snafu put the bottle down for a second and handed the card over to John. "Well, when I got the card, the teller told me I could get three hundred a day out. But every time I go to get the money, it says 'insufficient funds'. No matter how many times I try to get that three hundred dollars, it's never there."

'This guy is a complete idiot,' thought John. "Maybe I can get it to work. What's your secret pin number?"

"Do I look dumb enough to tell you my secret number is one - two - three - four? I don't think so."

"Please don't ask me questions like that," John answered. "My mother told me not to be rude to people."

John slid the debit card into the ATM machine and punched in Snafu's secret number. The machine was quiet for a moment and then it did something that John had never seen before...it started to laugh at him. The machine laughed hysterically for a good five minutes before the sounds died down to just a light giggle. Once the machine had ceased its snickering, a voice could be heard coming from the machine. "You want some money? Try getting a job, you freeloading scab off of a bitch's ass! Maybe then your account wouldn't be in the negatives."

John put his hand in his pocket, pulled out his wallet and started to count his cash. He looked at Snafu and shook his head sadly, then handed Snafu all of his money. "Here. Take this."

"What's this for?" Snafu asked as he took the money, then quickly put his hands back in the air.

"I don't know," said John. "A brain transplant...buy a balloon maybe. Hell, I just figure if the ATM laughs at you, then you're probably in worse shape than I am."

"Thanks." Snafu smiled "Beer fund."

John turned to leave but only got as far as the corner before glancing back for one final look at Snafu. John shook his head and yelled "You can put your hands down now and go home! This concludes the robbery!"

"Whew," Snafu responded. "That was a close call."

John disappeared into the alley without another word and immediately began banging his head into the brick wall, hoping to knock out all memory of the night's encounter.

•

The next morning, Snafu woke up naked and lying beside his neighbor Sally, who thankfully wasn't naked...she still had on one red sock. Snafu threw up, farted and pulled himself out of bed as quietly as he could. He started to grab his clothes off of the floor, heard Sally begin to wake up and decided that he could sacrifice the clothes...after all, he wasn't that attached to them. He grabbed the other red sock to use as a cock sock in order to protect what little pride he had, and left with his keys and cell phone in hand.

Snafu walked across the yards of the few trailers that separated his home from Sally's. General Nuisance was waiting for him on his doorstep with two cups of coffee. "Please tell me that's not your new costume."

Snafu smirked, turned his back towards his friend, and picked up the newspaper. "Oh dear Lord, that was a sight I did not need to see! For that matter, I'm not sure anyone needed to see it." Snafu unlocked his front door, walked into his living room and found Tripod stretched out on the couch. The cat looked up at Snafu, raised a paw in greeting and promptly threw up. He then farted and got down off the couch to follow Snafu into the kitchen. "See!" said the General. "I told you no one needs to see you like this." Snafu grunted and opened a cabinet next to the fridge. Remembering he was out of Kittie Kibble, Snafu opened a can of sardines and bent over to empty it into Tripod's food bowl. The cat immediately began to eat. Snafu put some water in another bowl and set it down on the floor. Tripod looked up as if to say 'what the hell is this shit?' "Don't look at me, man. You're the one who finished off the Tequila. You left the empty bottle on the floor again, I see. I've told you not to do that shit."Tripod let out a short growl and lowered his head to the water bowl. After a few dry heaves, he took a drink and went back to his sardines.

Snafu turned around, followed the General back out to

the porch and sat down on the steps beside his friend. General Nuisance moved over a few feet, then handed Snafu a cup of coffee. "Here. I got ya a cup of coffee."

"Oh man, thanks." Snafu took the cup with a smile, knowing that, in just a few brief seconds, his day would be getting much better. Snafu took a big sip, gagged, and sprayed the hot liquid on the ground in front of him. The look of disgust on his face was obvious. "What the hell is this?"

"It's a double cinnamon caramel mint espresso."

"Double caramel cinnamon mint? Dude, I thought you were picking us up coffee."

"It is coffee. What are you talking about?" laughed General Nuisance.

Snafu put the cup down. "Dude, I'm telling you, double caramel cinnamon mint espresso is not coffee. Coffee is coffee flavored, not this shit."

"It's the bestselling flavor at the Coffee Shack," replied General Nuisance.

"But did you see anyone ordering it?"

"Plenty of people," answered General Nuisance, as he took a sip of his own double cinnamon caramel mint espresso.

"I'm telling you, no true coffee lover would have ordered

this shit," scoffed Snafu.

"Seriously? Now you're a coffee connoisseur?" General Nuisance just shook his head.

"We're talking about the juice of life here and you are degrading it with all of these nasty flavors that make it taste like ass." Snafu stood up.

General Nuisance turned his face so that he was not staring at Snafu's junk which, now that his friend was standing, was uncomfortably at eye level. "And how would you know what ass tastes like?" He set his coffee down on the floor, primarily to give himself somewhere to look besides up.

Snafu lowered his head in shame. "Let's just say I've done some things in my life I'm not so proud of. But none of those things come close to equaling the abomination that is in this cup that you tried to pass off as coffee."

"Hate to tell you this, but you're in the minority. Most people love flavored coffees," laughed General Nuisance.

"But that doesn't make it right."

"It doesn't make it wrong either."

Snafu shook his head in disbelief. "In this case, yes it does. OK, let's put it this way...the other day I walked into a convenience store. I picked up a jar of Vaseline, asked the clerk for a men's magazine, and then after I payed for my stuff, I asked for the key to the bathroom."

"What the fuck is wrong with you?" asked General Nuisance. "Why would you do that? And what the hell does this have to do with the coffee?"

"Nothing is wrong with me. OK, maybe a few things...but that has nothing to do with this conversation," answered Snafu. "However, my analogy has everything to do with the coffee, which I'll get to in a minute. But I did it because I had to use the bathroom and would you believe the guy said 'no'?"

"Well, yeah...I mean it looked like you were going to yank your chicken in his bathroom. I don't blame him for saying no. I'd have said no too...maybe even 'hell no'!"

"Well I wasn't, but it proves my point about the coffee."

General Nuisance threw his hands up, as if to signal his confusion. "How does you beating your meat prove anything about coffee?"

"Flavored coffee and beating off in public are both the same. Just because you can do it doesn't mean you should," explained Snafu.

•

The Evil Overlord got out of bed, put on his fuzzy slippers, checked the telescope, saw that General Nuisance and Snafu were gone, cursed himself for leaving Da Bad Guy on watch detail, and went in to make a pot of coffee. He looked at the different flavors they had in the cabinet, finally deciding on double cinnamon caramel mint espresso. The aroma of the brewing coffee was enough to wake up Da Bad Guy.

The Evil Overlord was rather perturbed. "Weren't you supposed to be on watch detail?"

"Kinda, sort of…maybe…yea," Da Bad Guy answered. "Is that double cinnamon caramel mint espresso I smell?"

"Yes."

"Cool! My favorite."

"When was the last time you saw our minion?" asked The Evil Overlord as he handed Da Bad Guy a cup of joe, assuming flavored coffee can be called by such a simple term. The Evil Overlord adjusted the belt on his silk robe then put his hand on his hip, waiting impatiently for Da Bad Guy to answer. Da Bad Guy looked up, stared at him for a moment, and then registered that The Evil Overlord had asked him a question.

"Oh...Ralph? He called and said he wasn't feeling like himself today and would be a few minutes late," answered Da Bad Guy.

As if on cue, the door opened and a hot, scantily clad girl with black hair and nice tits walked in. The Evil Overlord and Da Bad Guy clinked their coffee cups together. "Today is looking up."

" Hey guys. Sorry I'm late," said the woman in a low, gravelly, altogether way too masculine voice.

"Who the hell are you?" barked The Evil Overlord as he tried not to stare at the lady's barely covered breasts...and not doing a good job of it.

"It's me...Ralph."

"No way you're Ralph! You're a chick...Ralph's a guy," laughed Da Bad Guy.

"Don't you think I know it? I went out on a date with this chick. Things didn't work out...she was a bit bitchy. Next thing I know, she's stalking me and shit. Well anyways, I pick up this young stripper and get her back to my place. Me and this stripper...well...we are getting all hot and heavy and then psycho chick busts in! At first I was like, 'Hot Damn, a threesome!' But she threw some powder on me and told me that, from this point forward, I would be a man trapped in a woman's body. When I woke up, the girls were both gone and I looked like this." Ralph cupped his now very large boobs and pushed them together and up.

"Dude, that really sucks," said Da Bad Guy.

"Parts of it does but I have to admit, these get to be fucking distracting," Ralph said as he fondled his large breasts.

"I can understand that. I mean hell, if I had some, I think I would probably stay home and play with them all day," admitted Da Bad Guy.

Ralph raised his eyebrow and winked. "Why do you think I was late?"

"They're not that nice," interrupted The Evil Overlord.

"Oh, please! Come on over and take these babies for a test drive." Ralph jiggled his breast at The Evil Overlord.

"Stop shaking those things at me!" The Evil Overlord screamed. "Can we just get back to talk of killing the heroes? After all, we do have a schedule to keep."

"You'd rather kill someone than play with boobs? What's wrong with you, man?" asked Da Bad Guy, shaking his head.

"Nothing...it's just that we have things to do." The Evil Overlord looked back and forth between his two sidekicks, who were both now staring at him as though he'd grown a third eye in the middle of his forehead. "Fine...OK. If it will shut you guys up so we can get back to work..."

The Evil Overlord crossed the room and took one breast in each hand. "Hey, those are pretty nice."

"Like those, do ya?" asked Ralph smiling.

"Have to admit I do," The Evil Overlord answered as he continued to fondle Ralph's boobs.

"So you like men, huh?"

"Hell no. Why would you say that?" asked The Evil Overlord.

"I don't know. Maybe because you're getting an erection rubbing on my boobs. I'm still a man, so cut it the fuck out. It's creepy!"

"But you told me to," protested The Evil Overlord as he took his hands off the boobs, giving each one final squeeze for the road.

"Well...he kinda expected you to say no," Da Bad Guy said as he took a sip from his double cinnamon caramel mint espresso.

"Oh...well, you know I was never very good at context clues. Can we just get back to planning out ways to kill those two?"

"Well, besides playing with the boobies, how is it?" asked Da Bad Guy. "I mean the whole being a woman thing."

"It is what it is, I guess. I mean, I miss scratching the old ball sack. Now when I stick my hand in my underwear to scratch them, they aren't there. The man part of me starts feeling my woman parts and I get turned on, but my female side of things says 'hell no, you haven't worked hard enough.' And then my other hand slaps me. Next thing I know, I'm all curled up in the fetal position...in bed crying, and I have no clue why."

The Evil Overlord face palmed himself. "Can we just change the subject? This is all rather disturbing."

"How the hell do you think I feel?" protested Ralph, starting to cry.

"Well, rather nice and firm...ah...I mean miserable...oh the hell with it! I'm going to go grab us some breakfast."

"But isn't that supposed to be my job?" asked Ralph.

"Normally yeah," answered The Evil Overlord, "but with the way this morning is starting out, I just need some alone time to gather my thoughts."

The Evil Overlord went to the sink, bleached his hands and scrubbed them with a metal cheese grater and then left without uttering another word.

The Evil Overlord strode purposefully down the street for several blocks before faltering when he noticed General Nuisance and Snafu approaching him. He quickly dipped down out of sight behind a trash can, patiently waiting for his two archnemeses to get closer. As they drew near, he launched himself from behind the trash can. "Ah hah! Now I have you!"

Snafu jumped back. "Oy, this is why I hate walking around in the city."

"Just give the bum a dollar and let's be on our way," muttered General Nuisance.

"What? I'm not a homeless person!" The Evil Overlord huffed indignantly.

"OK, you're an 'Urban Camper.' It's OK, I'm not judging," said Snafu as he made quote marks in the air with his hands. "Soup kitchen closes for breakfast at nine. If you hurry, I bet you can still make it."

"I'm a supervillain, set to spoil your plans of goodwill!"

Snafu turned to General Nuisance. "Every Comic-Con, these crazies come out of the woodwork."

"Yeah, either that or they are just whacked out on drugs. Sir, did you take anything? If you did, we can call 911 for you."

"Enough! Time to kill you with my slayer sword!" The Evil Overlord reached for the hilt that was usually at his waist, only to discover he didn't have it. "Shit! I can't believe I left the slayer sword at home!"

"Hmmm...Snafu this guy might be serious."

"You might be right; he could really be a-"

"LOOK! He's wearing girl boots!" General Nuisance interrupted.

"These aren't girl boots!!!" protested The Evil Overlord.

"They totally are...They're adore-a-boots!"

"That's it, my henchmen are about to kick your ass!" The Evil Overlord looked around for his henchmen. "That's the cue!" Still no henchmen. "Guys, you're supposed to jump out and help me now."

Snafu held out twenty dollars to The Evil Overlord. "Here you go. Take the twenty...looks like you need it more than we do...and please, PLEASE spend it on food instead of another fix."

The Evil Overlord fell to his knees, sobbing.

"God bless you; things will turn around for ya, little buddy," General Nuisance said as he patted The Evil Overlord on the top of his head.

General Nuisance turned to Snafu as they walked away. "See, I doubt those superheroes that live in New York have time for the little guys like we just helped out back there."

"Well, when you're right, you're right. I mean he did look pretty pathetic," Snafu agreed.

"Maybe at first, but when you handed him that money, those were tears of joy; I can tell you that for sure. Not sure if I've ever seen someone that happy in my entire life."

Snafu wiped a tear from his eye. "The whole world would be a better place if more people looked out for each other like that."

CHAPTER 5
Ticklewigglejigglepickle

"Hey, did you see the thing on the internet about the smallest penis competition they hold each year in New York?" Snafu set his beer down in his lap.

"Bullshit! No way there is a small penis competition. If there was, you would have entered and won every year!" laughed General Nuisance.

"Not true! I entered the last two years and came in dead last both years," quipped Snafu. "By several inches, I might add."

"More like you wish you could add a couple of inches."

"Hell, like you don't?"

General Nuisance took a puff of his Rolling Thunder 50 Caliber cigar. "If I had any more, I wouldn't be allowed to wear shorts because it would hang out of them."

"I wish!" his wife mumbled as she took a load of groceries in from the car.

"Must be wearing those short shorts from the seventies, huh?" Snafu replied with a shit eating grin on his face.

"Fuck you!" The General laughed. "My dick is so big it has its own zip code."

"Yeah right. Your shit's so small it earned you the nickname 'quarter inch killer' in high school."

"Hell, I wish it was that long. Having sex with you feels like you are just poking a little fun at me," his wife mumbled as she struggled to open the door with an armload of bags.

"A nice little rumor you started, if I recall," General Nuisance said as he tapped bottles with Snafu.

"Indeed I did."

"Ah, the amount of time I've had to prove that one wrong," General Nuisance said with a grin.

"And the more you tried to prove it wrong, the more it was proven correct." Snafu took a sip of his beer.

"Fuck you, you little prick! I've got TEN inches of limp dick."

"Well, you had better pull it out of your ass then, because it belongs to someone else!" Snafu nodded his head in the direction of General Nuisance's wife.

•

Meanwhile, across the street, The Evil Overlord and Da Bad Guy were monitoring the situation, waiting for their chance to strike.

"What are they doing now?" The Evil Overlord asked as he munched on his sandwich.

Da Bad Guy looked up from the telescope. "Well...it appears they are talking about the size of General Nuisance's package."

The Evil Overlord moved over to the window. "Let me see this package."

"What the hell is wrong with you? Why would you want to see another man's package?" Da Bad Guy just shook his head as he looked at his partner in crime.

"Oh, you mean THAT package?" The Evil Overlord looked a little embarrassed. "I thought you were talking about, you know, maybe a postal package."

"Man, you have to get your head back in the game. First you were getting a hard-on feeling up on Ralph, and now you want to look at General Nuisance's package — which according to him is almost a foot in length, assuming this baby monitor is working right."

"Damn, really? Ah...I mean, yeah right." The Evil Overlord looked down at his own package sadly and shook his head.

"But according to his wife and Snafu Fubar, that might be a fabrication of the truth," added Da Bad Guy.

"How would Fubar know how long the General's wee wee is?"

"Just call it a cock, big guy. We don't need no baby talk in the old hideout," Ralph said as he/she walked by in nothing but a thong.

"I'm pretty sure you're out of uniform," The Evil Overlord sputtered, as he tried to avert his eyes but found it rather hard to do.

"And I'm pretty sure you're staring at my tits again," snarled Ralph. "Want to feel me up again or are we over that part of the day?"

"Just get some clothes on, please." The Evil Overlord looked even more uncomfortable.

"No wonder I don't feel special anymore!" Ralph stormed from the room while imitating The Evil Overlord's voice. "Just go throw on some clothes...anything will do."

"Ah, see what you did? You hurt her feelings," said Da Bad Guy.

The Evil Overlord face palmed himself. "It's not a girl! It... Ralph...our minion...we are supposed to hurt his feelings and treat him like shit! It's all part of the contract."

"Oh yeah, I forgot," Da Bad Guy admitted. "Got distracted by the boobs."

"Can we please discuss anything except Ralph's boobs," pleaded The Evil Overlord.

"Sure. What did you have in mind? General Nuisance's wee wee?"

"Oh sweet Jesus, no! Just shut up and tell me what they are doing now."

"I can't properly shut up and tell you what they are doing at the same time, now can I? Well, unless of course I use sign language, which, of course I don't know," smirked Da

Bad Guy.

"You know what I mean," growled The Evil Overlord.

"Well, there appears to be a man in a cheap plastic alien mask walking up to them."

"What the hell?" The Evil Overlord looked astonished. "Let me see that."

The Evil Overlord pushed Da Bad Guy to one side as he looked through the telescope. "It could be a real alien you know."

"No way. You can even see the stretchy string holding the mask on. Look around the ear level," answered Da Bad Guy.

"Ah yes, I see that now."

•

"Dude, what the Hell is that?" General Nuisance looked at the stranger approaching them.

"No clue. Looks like a kid who thinks it is still Halloween," replied Snafu. He shook his head from side to side as he looked at what he assumed to be Peter wearing a cheap alien

Halloween costume.

"I'm no mere mortal child out dressing up for free candy, although I have to admit, free chocolate does have some potential." Snafu and General Nuisance nodded their heads in agreement. "My planet was being destroyed, so my parents stuck me on a space craft and sent me to your planet in hope of saving my life. Little did they know that your sun would give me great powers."

Snafu interrupted him. "That's ridiculous! I don't even have a son and even if I did, why the fuck would he give you any kind of special powers? If he was going to give powers to anyone, he would give them to me. After all, I'm his fictional daddy."

"Yeah, he has a point. I mean why the hell would his son that doesn't exist give you super powers? I mean, that just doesn't make any sense at all," chimed in General Nuisance.

"The sun, you fucking retard! The big yellow thing in the fucking sky. How fucking stupid are you two?" The newcomer shook with rage as he yelled at them.

"Do you really want me to answer that question?" asked Snafu.

The visitor dropped his head. "No...not really."

"Anyways kid...look, we don't have any candy," General Nuisance said.

"Why would I want candy when I'm an alien from a different planet? I have decided to conquer your planet, starting with the two of you."

"Shut the fuck up! You're not an alien...you're just some fucking dude wearing a plastic alien mask," laughed Snafu. "Why not kick back and have a few beers?"

"No seriously, I'm an alien, here to conquer you...and I don't want any of your disgusting beer."

"Hey, say what you want to about our planet but let's leave beer out of this," said Snafu. "Besides dude, I can see the fucking string holding the mask on to your face."

"That's part of my face you idiot. Ah, the hell with this...prepare to die!"

The pseudo-alien reached for something in his pocket, forcing the not-so-dynamic duo to spring into action (and yes, spring may be way too strong of a word...more like stumble across the porch into action, but that sounds nowhere near as heroic).

A short while later, the semi-heroes returned to their seats. "I kinda feel sorry for the little fellow," mumbled

Snafu as he pulled two more cold beers out of the cooler.

"You shouldn't. Hell, I thought it was a mask too. Not to mention, the EMTs said they should be able to reattach it to his face and, with some intense therapy, they expect him to make a full recovery and be back to conquering the earth in no time flat," General Nuisance replied as he took the beer. "Besides, you can't go up to the two most powerful heroes in the world and make those kind of comments and think we are going to sit idly by."

"True," answered Snafu. "Luckily he made those comments to us and not the guys you are talking about."

•

"It appears that another moronic attempt at vigilante justice has unfolded at the idiotic hands of General Nuisance and Snafu Fubar tonight."

Snafu flipped to another channel. "Man, I hate that guy. Oh, 'The Real Housewives of Clapton, North Dakota' is on."

"I know, that guy sucks...and to think I internet voted him the top news leader in the city and I could have voted for that guy who dresses up in the giant banana suit."

"Oh, not me! I voted for the giant yellow cock," laughed Snafu.

"Yeah, giant cock sounds right down your alley...your back alley, that is!" General gave Snafu a friendly punch on the arm.

"Yeah, yeah, whatever," Snafu said as he took a sip of his beer. "I just wish there was a way we could, you know, convince that news reporter that we're cool. Get some good press going for all of this hard work we do?"

"Good luck with that one," replied General Nuisance as he adjusted his package. "I think he would rather punch us in the old ball sack than talk good about us."

"Yeah, I agree. If only he had a weakness."

"Well, I did hear that he's a total poon hound with some very questionable and relaxed standards when it comes to the quality of chicks he bangs."

Snafu jumped up from his chair excitedly. "YOU MAGNIFICENT bastard, that's it!"

"That's what?" asked General Nuisance in bewilderment, while watching his friend dance around like an idiot. "I'm not going to let your toothless mother fuck him. That's taking too much for the team. Or in this case, taking too little for the team, if you know what I mean."

"No, you idiot! We can dress up like women and tell him how cool we think this dynamic duo of heroes are that protect our city." Snafu continued jumping around, almost spilling his beer.

"I don't like where this is going," General Nuisance responded slowly. "I mean, I always said I'd wait until prison to be fucked by a dude. Now, what you do in your own spare time is your own business."

"What the holy hell is wrong with you? That's gross," answered Snafu. "We're not going to have sex with him...at least I'm not...you? Well, that's an entirely different story. Besides, I could do better than that dinosaur. We're just going to get a few drinks in him and, you know, win him over to team Snafu and the General.

"Dude, he will never fall for that! I mean, hell, I have facial hair!"

"Just tell him you're Italian or German and that you forgot to bleach." Snafu started rubbing his hands together, his mind racing.

"He'll never believe we're women. I'm not going to do it.

Nope, not ever. Not even for the cause. Nope, nope, nope."

A FEW HOURS LATER...

Snafu leaned against the light pole in the parking lot of the TV studio, in what he considered a seductive pose. He was dressed in a tiger print mini skirt and a hot pink tube top (which barely covered "D cup" boobs) and was wobbling on stripper heels. He had on an extraordinary amount of makeup and sported a platinum blond wig.

General Nuisance tried to stay out of sight as much as possible. He looked positively conservative in comparison, wearing a short red dress with "A cup" boobs, a red wig, and clown-like make up.

"How come I get the small boobs?"

"Oh, be serious. You know we don't know what he's into, so we've gotta have a range of offerings."

"If he's not into big boobs, then we should have dressed like that old disco group with the cop and the Indian, cause he's into dudes at that point," laughed General Nuisance.

"No doubt."

James stormed out of the TV studio door, shouting behind him as he exited. "I was big when you punks were still crapping in diapers! How dare you speak to me that way! Tomorrow you'll be cleaning my toilet with your tongues!!!"

"Good, he's pissed. That will make this easier," said Snafu as he shifted his voice to that of a high pitched woman. "Oh, mister TV man."

James paused and stared at Snafu and General Nuisance in confusion. "What? Huh? Who are you?"

"Why, only your biggest fans," snickered Snafu.

"Groupies? Wow, it's been twenty years. I knew they'd come back." James straightened his tie and pushed his chest out a little bit.

"It's so exciting to finally meet you." General Nuisance stumbled over his high heels and leaned on James' shoulder."We're MILFs...and that "M" could stand for a couple of things."

"Like what?" asked James, as he thought about how dark the room would have to be before these women were attractive.

"Never mind that, sugar. Are you ready to party?"

"If by 'party' you mean me pay you for sex, I'm sorry,

but they don't pay me what you think they pay me. I mean, I live in an apartment with a cat and there's some Hungarian dude in the apartment below me. You have any idea what that is like?"

"If I say 'yes', does your story end?" asked General Nuisance hopefully. "If so...yes."

"It's hell, baby," James whined.

"Guess not." General Nuisance hung his head, resigning himself to hearing more about the anchorman's home life.

"All this weird music and fucking soccer. Do you know how much soccer that fucking Hungarian watches?"

"I don't know, baby....please tell us more!" General Nuisance shot Snafu an annoyed look but Snafu ignored him.

"ANYWAYS...no, baby...we're not hookers; we just want to hang out with you. Talk about all the coverage you've been giving to Snafu and General Nuisance."

"Huh? Oh, those two." James looked around to make sure no one else was eavesdropping. "Can you two keep a secret?"

"I knew it! You totally like sucking dudes off!" General Nuisance screamed.

"What!?! Oh, hell no! Where did you get that from?" James responded as he saw a couple on the other side of the street give them strange looks before hurrying off.

"Forgive my sister, she's a big fat virgin who doesn't know how to satisfy a man's need...to talk about himself..." interrupted Snafu.

"Oh, OK, no harm done...where was I? Oh right, my secret. I actually think those guys are cool."

A broad smile crossed the faces of Snafu and General Nuisance.

"Then you should say that on air, baby-kins!" Snafu said, trying his best but failing to sound like a sexy woman.

"I know, right? But it's all about those holy ratings. They have my hands tied..."

"Maybe I'd like to tie your hands," Snafu answered.

"Yeah, so we can punch you in the fucking sack!" added General Nuisance.

"What the hell?"

"Uh, she said so we can jump you in the fucking sack!" Snafu made a quick recovery as he glared at General Nuisance.

"Oh, OK, yeah that sounds much better."

"But before we get busy, tell us who you like better...General Nuisance or Snafu Fubar.

"General Nuisance," James answered without hesitation.

"But...but...but what about Snafu?" whined Snafu.

"I don't know. I mean, General Nuisance is a born leader. Snafu's just some love starved puppy in the shadow of greatness."

"Ha-ha...he called you a puppy."

"Shut up! But Snafu is cool too." Snafu was almost pleading as he felt his anger rising.

"Nah, not seeing it. He's just a prick. Did you see his costume the other day?"

"I know, right? Total shitville! It's like he was trying out for worst dressed wanna-be superhero or something." General Nuisance slapped James on the back as they both laughed.

"HEY! You said that costume was OK!"

"OK for a homeless dude maybe, am I right?" General Nuisance and James gave each other a high five.

"Let's get going...say, where's your car?" Snafu asked as he paced back and forth.

"It's that 1978 Ford Pinto over there...shall we..." answered James, still laughing and wiping his eyes.

"Looks a little dirty," Snafu sniffed as he walked around

the car.

"What are you doing?! This guy is totally into me...I'm not going to let you mess this up," whispered General Nuisance.

"Ladies, ladies, no need to fight...there's plenty of James to go around."

"I sincerely doubt that," muttered Snafu. "Hey, sugar, how about I give your car a bath?"

"I'd rather you sponge bathe me."

Snafu climbed up on the hood, hiked up his mini skirt and started peeing on the car, while at the top of his lungs singing, "At the car wash, baby! Workin' at the car wash..."

"You're a dude! I mean, that's not quite the deal breaker you'd think it'd be, but YOU'RE A DUDE!"

"Dammit, Snafu, I finally meet someone who 'gets' me and you screw it all up...I hate you! I hate you!"

The Evil Overlord stepped out of the dark alley behind the studio. "Now, Snafu and General Nuisance, I have you in my clutches."

"Gross, I don't want to be anywhere near his clutches," responded General Nuisance as he backed up a few feet.

"What do you think the word 'clutches' means?" Snafu narrowed his eyes at his friend.

"Figured it was a prison term for..." General Nuisance stopped, looked at The Evil Overlord, then James, and then whispered into Snafu's ear.

"What the fuck is wrong with you! It doesn't mean THAT! It means to have someone under your control." Snafu shook his head. "You know...sometimes I think you're just a fucking idiot."

"Focus, people," The Evil Overlord said rather sternly.

"Do people really say 'clutches'?" asked General Nuisance.

"Yeah, personally I would have gone with 'in my grasp' or 'under my thumb'," said Snafu.

"Is 'under my thumb' a prison term for..."

"No! Jesus, why is everything a prison term for gay sex with you?"

"I watch a lot of late night pay-per-view." General Nuisance shrugged his shoulders.

"OK, enough!If you'll direct your attention to my presentation." General Nuisance and Snafu watched as The Evil Overlord's henchmen finished setting up a projector.

"Arrg! He's going to kill us with a multimedia production." Snafu face palmed himself. "This really does suck!"

The first slide showed a picture of a very poorly drawn kitten. Under it was text that read:

My Plans to Take Over the City, A Primer Course,

by The Evil Overlord,
Produced by The Evil Overlord,

Views expressed in this presentation
do not reflect those of Evil Corp.
All Rights Reserved

"Isn't it a liability to disclose your plan to us? I mean, what if we get away?" asked General Nuisance.

"I don't follow you," said The Evil Overlord.

"He's saying if you give us a detailed outline of your plans and we escape, we'll be able to stop you," added Snafu.

"Come again?" The Evil Overlord looked confused.

"Aren't you going to tell us how you plan to take over the city?" General Nuisance spoke very slowly and carefully enunciated each word.

The Evil Overlord's eyes brightened in comprehension and he gave a resounding, "Yes! Yes, I am!"

"But what if we use that very knowledge to thwart your

plans?" asked Snafu.

General Nuisance started to open his mouth but Snafu cut him off. "And no, 'thwart' isn't a prison term!"

"Oh, how ironic. My very bragging would be my undoing. Does this happen a lot?" asked The Evil Overlord.

"Really?" General Nuisance shook his head in disbelief.

"I was home schooled. Mommy was a stripper. I didn't get to watch any TV." The Evil Overlord looked around. "So you probably don't want to see my presentation then, huh?"

"No!" Snafu and General Nuisance answered in unison.

"Fine! Gather up our stuff," The Evil Overlord ordered his henchman. "We are leaving."

"Hey, where did James go?" General Nuisance looked around quizzically.

"Guess he had better things to do," answered Snafu as they watched The Evil Overlord walk away in a huff.

Snafu Fubar and General Nuisance made the long trek home to Snafu's trailer, only to find Tripod stretched out in the dirt between an empty tequila bottle and what appeared to be one of the cats from the trailer next door. He was snoring. 'Damn,' Snafu thought to himself as he stepped over the cats to get to his front door. 'He's getting more pussy than I am!' Snafu shook his head. A few minutes later, he and General Nuisance were returning to their true state of being...or at least trying to.

"Hey, toss me another beer," General Nuisance said as he started to wash the makeup off of his face.

Snafu set a beer on the counter beside his friend, took a swig of his own, and turned on the news, only to see James' picture front and center.

"Cross-dressing trannies or dumb vagrants who piss on cars?" James smiled a wicked smile. "You decide. The story at 10."

General Nuisance and Snafu slumped down in the chairs by the cooler of beer. "Told you it was a stupid idea."

Snafu just nodded his head in agreement.

CHAPTER 6
Stroke the One-Eyed Burping Gecko

"In other news, two state college students were admitted to the emergency room tonight for alcohol poisoning." James' face wore a sly expression. "Apparently they were butt chugging. It is my guess that they are friends of General Nuisance and Snafu Fubar."

"What the hell is butt chugging?" General Nuisance popped the tops on two more beers.

Snafu looked up as he took the beer, then back at the TV. "How the hell would I know? I never went to college and had those wild party experiences like you did."

"Although the students involved denied they were butt chugging, several witnesses have confirmed that they did indeed see the students drop their pants and lie flat on the floor, their legs high in the air, while another student inserted a rubber hose with a funnel into their rectums. Students then poured alcohol into it. Sounds like butt chugging to me!"

Snafu and General Nuisance both lowered their beers in unison. "Did he say what I just thought he said?"

"That people are shoving a tube up their ass in order to get drunk?"

"Yeah, that's what I got from that too." General Nuisance looked at his beer and then at Snafu. "That's pretty bad."

"I mean, how do you even go about that?" Snafu quipped. "Hey buddy...you and I have been friends for a while and we both love to get drunk, so I'm going to take this plastic tube here and shove it up your ass. Oh, no, don't worry about me having to look at your fat hairy ass or nut sack. We are friends...that's all cool."

"Yeah, I just don't believe I'm that good of friends with anybody, especially not you," laughed General Nuisance. "I mean, I guess if my wife was into it...OK, maybe not my wife, but some fine chick—"

"I can hear you, asshole!" his wife screamed from the house. This was quickly followed by "Give it to me, Jim! You know just how mama likes it."

"Sounds like she is getting a little butt chugging of her own," Snafu said as he lit a cigar.

General Nuisance took the lighter and lit his cigar. "Nah, she is acting like she is having sex with the neighbor in an attempt to make me jealous so that I stay home and play house hubby instead of defending our fair city."

"Oh my god, Jim, you're hung like a fucking mule and know how to use it to make momma happy!" screamed Nuisance's wife.

"Some women will do anything to control their man." Snafu winced as he took another sip of beer. "Glad you're not falling for it."

"Oh yes! That tongue of yours is going to push me over the edge!"

"Yeah, I'm not that stupid. I know the truth." General Nuisance blew out a puff of smoke. "She's really in there with that ugly girlfriend of hers again, hoping I will come in and join them for a threesome."

Snafu held his beer up toward his friend. "Hats off to you, my friend. A weaker man would have shirked their duties and gone for the threesome."

•

"So what are they talking about now?" The Evil Overlord asked as he sat down beside Da Bad Guy, who was looking through the telescope and listening to the baby monitor, the other end of which was hidden in The Fucking Nuisance Cave.

"Butt chugging."

This caught The Evil Overlord's attention immediately. "Come again?"

"Butt chugging."

"I was afraid you said that." The Evil Overlord shook his head. "Never did get the idea behind that."

"Well, supposedly the alcohol gets into the system faster that way," Da Bad Guy replied without looking up.

"Sad day for society when slamming a few shots is just way too much effort." The Evil Overlord shook his head. "So how do you suppose that works?"

"What do you mean?" Da Bad Guy asked, looking up suspiciously.

"Well...I mean you're at a party, right? And someone goes 'Hey, we all know each other well enough, let's drop our drawers and butt chug.' But then they realize they only have one hose. Do they wash it in between or –"

"Seriously, just be quiet. I mean stop talking." Da Bad Guy walked out of the room, completely disgusted and feeling like he was about to blow chunks.

"Hey, I was just asking! Not like I've ever done it before. I thought maybe you might have more experience in this type of thing than me."

Da Bad Guy came back into the room. "Why would you think I'd have more experience in something like this than you? Do I look like someone who would stick a rubber tube up my ass just to get drunk?"

The Evil Overlord started to nod his head yes, but then thought better of it. "Ah no...not at all...my bad."

"Hey, Da Bad Guy, I've got the tequila, the funnel and the rubber tube you sent me out for," Ralph said as he entered the room. Ralph had finally put clothes on...black fishnet stockings, a super-short denim mini skirt, red stilettos, and a tank top. A bunny adorning the shirt was embellished with what looked like rhinestones. The Evil Overlord felt his dick harden.

"Don't judge me," Da Bad Guy said as he guided Ralph into another room.

The Evil Overlord breathed a sigh of relief as they vanished into the other room. He walked over to the telescope and decided to see what his two enemies were up to, thinking to himself, 'Man, I really need to get a grip!'

•

"So, you ever want to do anything other than be a super-hero?" General Nuisance asked as he got up to get two more beers.

"Well, at one time I kicked around writing erotica for like, one of them there romance novels." Snafu clipped the ends off of two *Córdoba & Morales* 19th Hole cigars, placing one where his friend could reach it. The other he stuck in his mouth and lit.

General Nuisance handed Snafu a beer. "YOU writing romance novels? That would be a kick to see." General Nuisance chuckled as he swallowed his beer, nearly choking in the process.

"Wouldn't it, though?" Snafu was nodding his head. "It would start off with 'Jimmy Billy Joe was in the garage, working on the Trans Am. He was bending over the hood, giving all the girls an eyeful of his nice hairy ass crack'."

"Sounds like you are in love," interrupted General Nuisance with a grin.

"Yeah, with your mom, so will you shut up and let daddy finish the story?" Snafu shook his head. "Now where was I? Oh yeah, Jimmy Billy Joe was working on his Mustang-"

"A second ago it was a Trans am," interrupted General Nuisance.

"See, this is what happens when you distract me. I can't keep the story straight." Snafu took a sip of his beer. "Can I continue, please?"

"Oh, please do."

"Jimmy Billy Joe was working on his TRANS AM, his beer belly covering the small chubby he had from cleaning the pistons. Nothing gets a man going like lubing his engine."

Snafu adjusted his crotch."Jimmy Billy Joe heard a moaning noise from behind him. He turned and watched as Ms. February stepped off of the calendar and stood buck ass naked in front of him. The next thing Jimmy Billy Joe knew, she was grinding her naked bare body up against his hot sexy beer belly that no longer was enough to conceal his redwood. Although he found the whole experience odd, he didn't give it a second thought...after all, she was Ms. February."

"Ms. February whispered into Jimmy Billy Joe's ear, 'Give it to me like they do in the movies'."

"Jimmy Billy Joe wiped his greasy hands on a rag before grabbing Ms. February by the hair, spinning her around, and bending her over the hood of the Mustang...ah...I mean Trans Am, and just tearing that ass up. It was at that moment that Ms. February realized that, although she was a made up fantasy, Jimmy Billy Joe watched entirely different kinds of movies than the chick flicks that Ms. February watched. Ms. February climbed back into the calendar, knowing she would not sit or shit right for a week. As for Jimmy Billy Joe, he pulled out the buffer and started to put a shine on his pride and joy."

"And by 'pride and joy', I hope you mean the car?" asked

General Nuisance.

"I think I would leave that to the reader's imagination."

"I agree. I always hate it when the writers spell every-thing out." General Nuisance took a sip of his beer. "I have to admit it; I owe you an apology. That was pretty good. I really thought it would be rather lame."

"We all have hidden talents," Snafu said as he took another puff on his cigar. "Mine is just turning words into arousal."

•

"What the hell?" asked Da Bad Guy as he staggered into the room where The Evil Overlord was. "Are you jerking off in our secret hideout!?!"

"Ah…well…ah yeah…kind of," answered The Evil Overlord as he pulled a towel over his waist to hide his junk. "I mean Snafu was telling an erotic story and I have to admit it sorta got me going."

"But couldn't you have gone to the bathroom for that? I mean HELL, this is where we work!" Da Bad Guy leaned against the wall. "Damn dude, there better not be anything sticky on the telescope."

"Oh, there won't be; I'll be sure to clean it up," answered The Evil Overlord sheepishly.

Da Bad Guy crossed the room to resume his watch. "Ah, I wouldn't sit there just yet," said The Evil Overlord.

"Please tell me you didn't shoot off on my seat."

"Maybe."

"I haven't butt chugged enough for this...I'll be back." Da Bad Guy grabbed a bottle of rum and left the room with Ralph in tow. Ralph was missing one of his stockings.

●

"I briefly kicked around the idea of being a priest," Snafu said as he farted. "Man, that was a wet one."

"And smelly," said General Nuisance as he fanned the air. "You? A priest? I just can't see that one."

"Yeah, well neither could the people in charge of the church," laughed Snafu. "Probably for the best. I mean, you know they don't allow you to drink unless it is wine and you know how wine gives me a headache."

"True...plus there is that whole no sex thing."

"Yeah, I know...well, unless you're into altar boys, which I'm not," Snafu replied looking uncomfortable. "I think the main reason they wouldn't let me in, though, were my religious beliefs...or lack there of...which is odd since they are not supposed to discriminate based on religion."

"Well, I would think that being of the same faith as the church you're trying to be a priest at would more or less be a requirement."

"Yeah, that's what I discovered," Snafu said as he scratched his balls.

"Besides, if you were a priest, you would probably be like that one I heard about in South America the other day," General Nuisance said.

Snafu looked up from his drink, shrugging his shoulders. "What priest?"

"Well, this priest convinced his followers that his semen was 'holy milk'."

"No fucking way," laughed Snafu. "Holy Cum...ingenious!"

"Oh, it gets better. He also had them believing the only

way to receive God into their lives was orally, so after worship service was over, he would take female members of the congregation into the back room for a quick blow job."

"No way."

"Can you believe they arrested him for this?"

"They should have arrested the people who thought sucking their priest's dick would get them into heaven...just for being stupid."

"Yeah, I can see the coffee shop banter on that one," added General Nuisance."My wife is a better person than your wife. The priest blesses her twice a day. Our good night kiss is kind of salty and sticky though."

"But could you imagine being part of his church? OK, General Nuisance. For you to get into heaven, you need to get down on your knees and bring forth the holy milk."

"Yeah, I'd be going to hell."

•

Da Bad Guy and Ralph staggered back into the room. "Anything new?" The Evil Overlord looked up to see Da Bad Guy and Ralph standing next to the counter. Da Bad Guy looked like he was about to fall down, so Ralph was holding onto him to help him stay upright. Ralph was now missing both stockings, his stilettos and the bunny tank top. The Evil Overlord turned back to the window quickly.

"Apparently Snafu wanted to be a priest."

"Well, thank goodness that didn't get you aroused," replied Ralph. "Would have hated to find you with your junk out while they were talking about altar boys."

"More awkward than him jerking off in our hideout?" asked Da Bad Guy.

"Ah, can we just move on to more current and pressing issues," interrupted The Evil Overlord, "like how are we going to find The Fucking Nuisance Cave and get rid of our archnemeses?"

"Once again, I'm pretty sure that IS The Fucking Nuisance Cave right down there," screamed Ralph, as he pointed out the window to where Snafu Fubar and General Nuisance sat enjoying a tasty ice cold beverage.

"Ralph, if you're not going to add anything useful to the conversation, please just shut the fuck up." The Evil Overlord got up and leaned against the window sill. "Finding the

Holy Grail would be easier than finding The Fucking Nuisance Cave."

"One, The Fucking Nuisance Cave is right in front of you and two, the Holy Grail doesn't exist."

Da Bad Guy and The Evil Overlord both stared at Ralph. "What do you mean, it doesn't exist? Haven't you seen all the movies made about it?"

"You do know they make movies about stuff that no longer, or never did, exist right?" Ralph shook his head in disbelief as he typed up something on the laptop. "Here is an online video that shows a reenactment of the last supper."

"Well, how do they know it's accurate?" asked Da Bad Guy.

"It's online. That means it has to be accurate."

"He has a point there," said The Evil Overlord.

"Just watch the damn video and shut up," said Ralph as he flipped the computer screen around so they could both see. On the computer screen was a man in a white suit. "What you are about to see is a reenactment of the last supper. Bear in mind, the last supper took place at what today would be the equivalent of a low cost family restaurant. There were many religions coming and going at the time, but

Jesus had gained a certain amount of fame and everywhere he went, people wanted to see him."

The camera on the computer screen zoomed into a private dining room where Jesus and his apostles were eating dinner.

"I say unto you, that one of you...what?!?" Jesus looked up at the clearly excited waiter who had just interrupted him.

"Can you pass me that water glass?"

"I'm in the middle of something here," Jesus replied as he handed the glass over.

The waiter filled the water glass, returning it to the table. "Listen, I don't mean to gush, but I'm a big fan."

Jesus sighed and gave Peter a go-to-Hell look. "Oh Peter, where's my advance prep? They should know, no photographs or signatures."

Peter let out a nervous laugh. "Hey, I was busy rounding up donkeys for you, remember? I couldn't do that AND get a PR package to these folks."

The waiter handed Jesus a menu. "Could you sign this for my niece? We saw your sermon on the hill...dynamite stuff."

Jesus pulled out a sharpie from his pocket. "Fine, what's

your niece's name?"

"Betty Lou."

Jesus paused and looked at the waiter. "Betty Lou? Really?OK, never mind." Jesus started to talk as he signed the menu. "To Betty Lou, your uncle really nailed me down to get me to sign this. Stay in school. Oh, and don't have relations with goats, you'll totally burn in Hell for that." Jesus stopped for a moment and looked at Paul. "That goes for you too by the way, buddy boy."

Paul hung his head. Christ began writing again. "Your Savior and best pal, Jesus Howard Christ."

"Oh, thank you! Thank you! Thank you!" The waiter danced around the table in delight.

"I think we're waiting on some bread sticks," Jesus interrupted.

The waiter sat down. "Listen, I could totally do this disciple thing with you."

The disciples groaned and rolled their eyes.

"Err...I'm not accepting resumes at this time, but I do have a little dead weight on my team, so you never know. Say, how are we doing on those bread sticks..."

"So can I give my resume to you, or is there an HR department I need to go through?

"Bread...sticks...right....freaking...now..." growled Jesus.

"Fine! Now I understand why they say don't meet your heroes," the waiter said as he stormed off.

"He's totally wiping his pee pee on those bread sticks," said Paul.

"Yeah, after he uses them to push his sweaty ball sack back and forth," added Peter.

"What? I think I handled that well...but yeah, I'm totally not eating those bread sticks when he brings them," replied Jesus.

The scene switched to the waiter cleaning up after the party. "I hope they liked nuts with their bread sticks."

The waiter took all of the dishes off of the table and dumped them into a camel drinking trough. One of the drinking glasses fell and shattered. "Dammit! That was Jesus' mug. I was going to give that to Betty Lou," said the waiter as he grabbed another mug out of the trough. "Oh well, I'll just give her this one...she will never know the difference."

"See, the Holy Grail was destroyed after the last supper. It no longer exists," said Ralph as he sat back in the recliner.

"Well dammit," said The Evil Overlord. "It's online so it must be true. Now we need to find a new plan."

"What if we found the original pieces and glued them back together?" asked Da Bad Guy.

"How bout we just order a fucking pizza instead," suggested Ralph.

Da Bad Guy and The Evil Overlord looked crestfallen but agreed that their dreams of owning the Holy Grail had slipped through their finger tips.

As Ralph ordered pizza, The Evil Overlord pulled a cup from the cupboard and poured himself some water. Written on the bottom of the cup was "To my biggest fan, Betty Lou. Love, Jesus Howard Christ."

CHAPTER 7
Tug the Slug

"So, I was at the Jerk Hut yesterday-"

"Why the hell do I need to know this?" interrupted General Nuisance. "I mean, granted, I don't think you should be going to places like that because quite frankly, if you get busted in a raid, it's not going to look good on us as a superhero duo. But I'm pretty sure I can distance myself from ya, at least in the media."

"I seriously doubt the media or anyone else is going to care that I stopped by the Jerk Hut," replied Snafu.

"You say that now, but celebrities and politicians always

meet their downfall in sex scandals."

"What the hell are you talking about?" asked Snafu as he got up to grab two more beers. "What does me going to the Jerk Hut have to do with a sex scandal?"

General Nuisance took the ice-cold beer from Snafu. "Well...did you play with your chicken while you were in there?"

"Well yeah, but it's not like anyone saw me. I mean, I took a booth in a corner so I was sort of out of sight," answered Snafu as he took a sip of his beer.

"Oh, trust me, someone saw you. You may not have seen them but someone saw you. They have cameras in those places. When you show up playing with your chicken on national TV, I'm going to claim you must have gone crazy or something like that." General Nuisance took a sip of his beer.

"Would it make you happy if I stayed away from the Jerk Hut?"

"It would make me extremely happy."

"Fine. Then I'll stay away from it, but you had better find me another place to get Jamaican jerk chicken because that was my favorite restaurant."

"Anything new on the location of their secret lair?" asked

The Evil Overlord as he re-entered the room.

"Nah," answered Ralph as he shoved a chocolate bar in his mouth. "Snafu was talking about visiting the Jerk Hut again."

"Oh really?" replied The Evil Overlord inquisitively. "Did he by chance mention, ah, where this jerk hut was located?"

"It's not that kind of jerk hut. It's a place to get Jamaican chicken, you perv."

"Ah, yes precisely. I knew that. I just, ah, really love Jamaican chicken," replied The Evil Overlord rather sheepishly.

"Only if by loving Jamaican chicken, you mean you love to beat off in our secret lair," interrupted Da Bad Guy.

"Like I'm the only one to ever jerk off in here." The Evil Overlord looked at Ralph and Da Bad Guy. Both were shaking their heads back and forth. "In that case, can we just move on and talk about something else? Like maybe something that doesn't include me jerking off?"

•

Snafu gave General Nuisance an odd look as a heavy set bearded man, wearing nothing but a polka dotted towel, waddled up the driveway. The man started to speak, but General Nuisance held up his hand, indicating that he needed to pause, which the man did.

General Nuisance and Snafu exchanged glances again and without a word, both grabbed two beers each from the cooler. Snafu offered two to the man in the polka dotted towel, but he replied 'I don't drink.' Snafu simply shook his head as he and General Nuisance both double fisted the beers until they were gone. They each grabbed two more beers, opened them, all the while looking at the man. "OK, you may continue now," said General Nuisance as he began to repeat the double fisting ritual.

"I'm here to join your group," said the man. "My friend, Peter, said you might be looking for a few new members."

"Yeah, probably not going to happen since you don't drink," General Nuisance said as he took another sip from both bottles. "Besides, you really don't look like much of a superhero. I mean, you have to have powers and a name, plus there is the whole costume thing. I mean, we are a little liberal on the costume, but we are also traditionalists in the sense that we would like you to have at least some sort of costume."

"Oh, I have a name and a costume," replied the man in the polka dotted towel. "I'm Super Wing Wong Dong Man. I have a huge dick, with a cape...wanna see?"

"Nah, I'm good," Snafu quickly answered, almost spewing his beer all over the man.

"You sure?"

"Yeah, I'm pretty sure we don't want to see your junk."

"But it has a cape."

"I don't give a fuck if it has a hat and a tie. I still don't want to see it," screamed Snafu.

"What the hell does it have a cape for?" interrupted General Nuisance. "I mean, doesn't it get caught in your zipper and shit?"

"It used to. That's why I just wear the towel now."

"Ah, that makes sense," chimed in Snafu. "And what superpower do you have?"

"It can shoot out a super sperm."

"Yep, conversation just went straight to the Ninth Plane of Hell." General Nuisance winced. "Why the hell did you think we would like to see your junk that shoots out super sperm?"

"Junk with a cape," added Snafu.

"Well, you're two guys hanging out. I just kinda figured you two were...well...kinda...you know?"

"No, we don't know," General Nuisance answered defensively. "Kinda what?"

"Well, you know...gay."

"Do we look fucking gay to you?" Snafu stood up angrily.

"Well yeah, kinda."

"This is coming from a fat man wearing a polka dotted towel who claims to have a cape on his cock. I'm sorry if we are not going to take your opinion too seriously. I think it's time you leave." General Nuisance turned his attention back to his ice cold, frost brewed, liquid love.

"But don't you want to see my cape? It's red."

"HELL NO!" yelled Snafu. "Just go home or something. Play in traffic. Maybe join the creepers in the building over there who keep watching us through the telescope. Just leave."

Super Wing Wong Dong Man walked down the driveway with more than his hopes drooping.

"Do you think they meant us when they were talking

about the creepers with the telescopes?" asked The Evil Overlord.

"Nope," answered Da Bad Guy. "We aren't creepers. We are supervillains, but we will need to keep the blinds pulled to make sure our privacy is not being violated."

"Hey, dumbass!" Snafu winced as he heard his neighbor's voice getting louder and closer. "Did you call that environmental group on me when I was sunbathing earlier?"

"Yeah...I ah...thought you were beached. I was just trying to get you back to your pod. Wait a minute...did you waddle all the way over here just to bitch at me?"

"You're an asshole!" she said as she knocked his beer out of his hand and stomped off down the driveway. She was wearing her black and white bikini that showed off entirely too much of her body. General Nuisance wasn't sure why, but he had a sudden urge to go to Ocean World.

Snafu got up angrily and picked up his beer bottle. "Whew, that was close. Thank God it was empty."

"Might as well grab us two more while you're up," General Nuisance said as he watched Sally lumber down the driveway. "It's kind of like a lava lamp. I just can't take my eyes off of it."

"Yeah, having sex with her is kinda like bull riding. You just slap her ass and see if you can hang on for eight seconds."

"So, have you ever made the whistle?" laughed General Nuisance as he took the beer from Snafu.

"Once or twice. I got game."

"No, what you got is big game...as in the elephant variety." General Nuisance finally managed to pull his eyes away from Sally. "And here I thought bestiality was illegal."

"Better be glad it's not, otherwise you'd never get laid."

"I'm married. I don't have to worry about getting laid," laughed General Nuisance.

"Yeah, because it ain't happening, asshole!" his wife screamed from inside the house. "Oh yeah, baby! Give it to mama, just like she likes it, you big stud!"

"Man, the way she tries to make me jealous is so cute." General Nuisance took another sip of his beer. "Hard to find a good, loyal woman like that these days."

•

"Do you think he is really that clueless as to his wife's sexual escapades?" asked Da Bad Guy as he listened to the baby monitor.

"Sadly, yes," answered Ralph from the other room. "He really doesn't seem that bright."

"Don't let him fool either of you," interrupted The Evil Overlord. "That's all a ruse to lure you into a false sense of security...right before he pounces on you, delivering a deathblow to your criminal careers."

"Maybe," said Da Bad Guy, "but I'm pretty sure they are just both fucking idiots who have to write 'breathe' on their hands with a sharpie so they don't forget to do it."

•

"So, what's the deal with you and Sally anyways? I mean you guys just friends with benefits or is it getting serious?"

"Nah, nothing like that. I mean, we hate each other, so definitely not that. More like enemies with benefits," replied Snafu. "Having sex with her is kind of like riding a scooter. It's fun and shit but you don't want your friends to know."

"So, basically you're married but living at different houses," said General Nuisance.

"Well, there is one difference. I mean, I actually get laid."

"Can't argue with you there."

•

"I've got it!" yelled The Evil Overlord from the bathroom, where he sat reading a magazine and answering Mother Nature's call. "Boys, come here. This is important."

Da Bad Guy and Ralph exchanged glances. "Ah, can it wait until you're out of the can? I mean, it sounds like you have been wrestling with a wet animal in there."

"Yeah, the smell ain't so great either," added Ralph. "Really don't want to be up close and personal with that smell unless we have to."

"Seriously guys, there's nothing wrong with taking a healthy dump," answered The Evil Overlord. "It's all part of the natural order of things."

"There's nothing natural about the smell coming from in there," responded Da Bad Guy as he frantically sprayed air freshener around the bathroom door. "More like a sewage leak. You sure things aren't backing up in there?"

The toilet flushed and The Evil Overlord exited the bathroom. Ralph was hanging his head out of the window, vainly hoping to get some fresh air. Da Bad Guy was holding a kitchen towel over his nose and had a fan pointing directly at his head to blow away the stench.

"I think you're being a little melodramatic."

"No, we're not," answered Ralph, pointing at a dead flower. "You wilted it."

"Oh wow...I did that?Yeah, OK, well I had some bad chili, OK? Give me a break," said The Evil Overlord. "So do you want to hear my idea or not?"

"I've already figured it out. We just give you some chili and lock them in the same room with you."

"Well, you're not too far off from what I was thinking."

"We can't do it," interrupted Ralph. "That's cruel and un-usual punishment. THEY don't even deserve that."

"We kidnap Nuisance's wife and tell him that if he ever wants to see her alive again, that he will tell us the location of The Fucking Nuisance Cave," snickered The Evil Overlord as he rubbed his hands together.

"So, who would we give the note to? Nuisance or the neighbor she's banging like a drum on the side?" asked Ralph with a slight grin. "I mean, the neighbor might actually pay to get her back."

"We're not after money. We want the location of The Fucking Nuisance Cave," said The Evil Overlord. "And if you say it's right down there in the driveway one more time, I swear to all that is holy I will hold you down and shit on you."

Ralph closed his mouth, keeping his thoughts to himself for fear that The Evil Overlord might actually carry out his most-vile threat.

•

"So, I waited in line for almost three hours before I got to audition for *Lost Hope Has Talent*." Snafu took a sip of his beer. "I was surprised there were that many people in line. I mean, let's face it, I've been to some talent shows in this town before and wasn't impressed."

"Well, maybe they were getting the footage of all the losers that try out...you know, to make the show more funny," General Nuisance said as he spied The Evil Overlord, Da Bad Guy and Ralph sneaking down the street. "Don't look now but it looks like we got some religious fanatics coming. Hope they go to the house and don't see us out here."

Snafu and General Nuisance watched as the three went around the corner of the house. "Whew! that was a close one. Now, back to what you were saying."

"So anyways, I wait three hours in line to audition and would you believe those bastards told me that fiddling the flesh flute was not a talent?"

"Have to admit it's nothing I really want to see."

"Yeah, they said it was nothing anyone would want to see," replied Snafu. "Although one of the creepy looking judges did give me his card and told me to call him."

Snafu and General Nuisance's conversation was interrupted when Jim came running out of the Nuisance house in nothing but his boxers. "They've taken your wife! They said that if you give them the location of The Fucking Nuisance Cave, they would return her."

General Nuisance stood up with a defiant look on his

face. "Nobody takes my wife and threatens to bring her back!"

Snafu's stomach rumbled. "Hope she made some sammiches before they took her." He looked around, feeling slightly guilty for thinking about food at a time like this.

"We can only hope." General Nuisance leaned in closer to Jim. "Did she make sammiches?"

"Yeah, that wasn't exactly what she was doing when they came into the house," Jim answered, feeling very uncomfortable having this conversation with his mistress's husband. "But they did say that the two of you should wait for them in the driveway or else you would never see her again."

Snafu walked over and checked the humidor. "Plenty of cigars."

"Beer's fine too." General Nuisance closed the cooler. "I guess there is only one thing to do."

•

"What the fuck do you mean they went for a walk?" The Evil Overlord grabbed Jim by his hair. "Did you give them the exact message...that we would kill her if they were not here?"

"Yes, they took the cigars and beer and went for a walk! What the hell was I supposed to do? Stop them?" Jim looked a little disheveled. "General Nuisance said something about them needing a little exercise."

"Oh good lord; Ralph tie him up," demanded Da Bad Guy. "Now what?"

"We wait." The Evil Overlord took a seat. "Even if it takes an eternity. We wait."

"Hey Ralph...honey...could you at least tie me and Jim up together? Preferably naked and facing each other?" Nuisance's wife batted her eyes at Ralph.

"Sure, why not? Might be entertaining in a sick, sad sort of way."

After several hours of the villains watching General Nuisance's wife and Jim do things that would make a sailor blush — or dissolve into tears — our drunken heroic duo returned to The Fucking Nuisance Cave. Beers in hand, cigars in mouth, ready to take care of business.

The trio of bad guys stood up, as if ready to fight, but Snafu walked right past them. "Where the hell is he going?" Da Bad

Guy threw down the deck of cards that he had been playing solitaire with.

General Nuisance let out a loud, long belch before responding. "He's got to take a leak. Usually he does it behind the shed, but since we have guests, he thought that would be rude."

"Never stopped him before!" Nuisance's wife was straddling Jim. "Oh mama loves it when you do that! Baby, you always do me right!"

Snafu emerged from the house with his zipper down. "We ready to do this thing?" Snafu and General Nuisance stood side by side, chests puffed out and arms linked together like a couple of dirty, overgrown kids about to play a game of Red Rover. General Nuisance spoke first.

"You three have kidnapped my wife and brought her back. Then you forced her and our dearly loyal and beloved neighbor into some sort of sick act of bondage sex for your own cheap amusement. Not to mention the lies you told about killing her if we did not wait for your arrival." General Nuisance took a step forward. "These deceitful acts cannot go unpunished!"

"Uh excuse me...is one of you the homeowner?" The battle that was brewing came to an abrupt halt. A tiny man was approaching, carrying a clipboard and wearing a wrinkled pinstripe suit that looked as if it might belong to a clown. "I'm Milton from the Detroit Potato Institute –"

"The what?" General Nuisance looked around the driveway and saw everyone shaking their heads or shrugging their shoulders as if to say 'I've got nothing'.

"Technically, I'm a Detroit Potato Institute Inspector, a DPI I if you will." Milton paused briefly as he noticed Jim and Nuisance's wife still going at it."Uh...that's sick!" Milton adjusted his tie while trying not to watch the couple who was now fornicating in a way that was...unnatural."The reason for my visit is...well to be perfectly honest with you...there has been an outbreak of fake potatoes being sold in your area. So now I'm forced to go house to house, witness some very sick shit, and inspect any potatoes that you might have in your possession." A muffled moan to his right again caught his attention. "And for the love of all that is holy, please tell me those two do not have a potato in their possession."

"Shouldn't you be out of Idaho? I mean, that is the potato state after all?" Snafu took a puff of his cigar.

121

"Curious story there. We were originally based in Idaho. However, once Detroit went bankrupt, we could get land and a building at pennies on the dollar, so like any good America-loving company, we took advantage of the poor and defenseless and reaped record financial gains." Milton smiled. "Made it easier to convince those senators to give us more government potato contracts."

"Ah, that's nice and all, Milton, but we're kind of in the middle of something here." General Nuisance put his arm around Milton to lead him back down the driveway.

"Doesn't really matter. As a DPI I, I'm obligated and have orders to inspect any potatoes that are on the premises." Milton held his ground, refusing to be directed down the driveway. "That would also include any potato type products, such as chips, fries...you get my drift."

Ralph dumped a bucket of cold water on the kinky couple and then turned to Milton with a concerned look on his face. "We just bought some potatoes the other day. Any chance when you're done here, you could check them out?"

"We will get to your house in due time." Milton removed General Nuisance's arm from around his shoulder. "Now, if you wouldn't mind, show me your potatoes."

"Well, if you insist." General Nuisance started to unzip his pants.

"'Show me your potatoes' is not prison slang for 'whip your junk out', you idiot!" Snafu screamed. General Nuisance zipped his pants back up. "Man, you've got to stop assuming everything you don't understand is a euphemism for prison sex. What the fuck is wrong with you?"

"I kinda sorta thought he meant the same thing." The Evil Overlord zipped his pants back up as well. "Simple misunderstanding really. Anyone could have made it."

General Nuisance's wife and Jim led Milton into the house. As the door closed, a battle of epic proportions was imminent.

CHAPTER 8
Teaching the Cyclops the Lambada

Milton watched the battle safely from inside General Nuisance's house. General Nuisance's wife brought out all of their potato products and dumped them on the kitchen floor for Milton's inspection, then she and Jim went back to doing what they did best. Both events were unlike anything that Milton had ever seen in all of his years as a Detroit Potato Institute Inspector. His training, as detailed as it had been, had not prepared him for anything like this.

Milton emerged from the house after witnessing things

that would make a maggot puke. He hoped that he would be able to drink enough to erase this day from his memory, but he feared there was not enough alcohol in the world for that.

Inside the house, Jim and General Nuisance's wife rolled around naked on the floor in what had now become potato salad. Never had Milton seen anyone make potato salad in quite such a fashion and if there was a loving God, he would never see it again.

Bodies lay motionless outside in the driveway. What had started off with Da Bad Guy grabbing Snafu's hand and yelling at the top of his lungs, "One, two, three, four; I declare a thumb war!" went tragically wrong when Snafu replied with "Five, six, seven, eight; that's the hand I use to masturbate!"

Da Bad Guy had tried to free his hand but Snafu had it in a death grip. There was nowhere to run, no escape. Snafu hit Da Bad Guy with his beer, sending the villain to the ground. A small tear rolled down Snafu's face as he watched the beer geyser into the air. As he pounced on Da Bad Guy, he tried to suck as much of the beer as he could out of his costume, but had to give up due to the pungent taste of sweat mixing in with the sweet taste of beer.

General Nuisance had poured two shots of rum, passed one to The Evil Overlord and pronounced, "Time to settle this like men." The two drank to the point that only General Nuisance remained standing, assuming you call leaning up against the workshop's wall standing.

Milton handed General Nuisance a piece of paper as he left. "Your official report will be in the mail to you in three to six weeks. Thank you for your cooperation."

"Oh, my baby! What happened to my baby?" Sally ran as fast as her large, tree trunk legs would carry her to where Snafu lay motionless on the ground.

General Nuisance called 911, then he finished securing the villains. "Hang on buddy! Help is on the way."

•

Tripod watched out the window as an ambulance passed his trailer, followed closely by General Nuisance's car. A vague thought that the source of his food supply might be in that ambulance concerned him somewhat. The cat took a swig from his bottle of Tequila, farted, then pulled up the internet and took out a 'room for rent' ad, just to be on the safe side.

•

General Nuisance sat quietly beside Sally in the hospital waiting room. The two had never spoken much to each other and neither saw the need to change that happy state of affairs now. General Nuisance had tried several times to get back to see his friend in ICU, but had been told no, that the situation was too dire. General Nuisance hated the thought that he might have to recruit Peter as his new side kick. He knew damn well it would NOT be the dude with the cape on his cock. That was just too creepy. He shuddered as the thought crossed his mind.

A doctor entered the nearly deserted waiting room and looked around before walking toward the General and Sally. "Are you his next of kin?"

"Only family the man has." General Nuisance stood up. "How is he, doc?"

"Got some bad news for you. He didn't make it." The doctor put a hand on General Nuisance's shoulder. "I'm sorry. We did all we could for him, but in the end we couldn't save him."

General Nuisance and Sally both fell to the floor in tears, screaming "NO!"

The doctor watched for a moment and then shook his head. "I'm just fucking with you. He's going to be OK."

"What the hell is wrong with you? You don't joke about shit like this." General Nuisance grabbed the doctor by his shirt collar.

"Just a little bedside humor."

"Very little," growled General Nuisance. "So is Snafu OK or not?"

"Oh, he's fine. It was a little bumpy in the beginning when the transfusion wouldn't take. We thought he had O negative blood. Turns out he was A positive...as in alcohol...so we just hooked an IV up to a keg...pepped him right up."

"That's my boy!" General Nuisance wiped away a tear of joy.

General Nuisance gave Snafu a hug when he entered the hospital room, a greeting which naturally was immediately followed by "No go homo."

"So what happened to the bad guys?"

General Nuisance unhooked Snafu's IV and took a few shots of the magical fluid of life before he declared, "Fear not, my friend. Justice has prevailed yet again and they are resting comfortably behind bars."

•

The evil trio woke up in a smelly alley, lying on a discarded mattress. "What the hell are we doing in an alley behind all of these strip clubs and bars?" The Evil Overlord grabbed Da Bad Guy's hand to help him up. Da Bad Guy got to his feet with difficulty and said, "Could be any number of reasons, but if I had to guess one, it would be that our archnemeses are fucking idiots." The three gathered themselves together and headed back to their secret lair to plan their next attack and hope that the location of The Fucking Nuisance Cave would one day be revealed.

THE END

ABOUT THE AUTHOR

Bob Dixon is a two-time Guinness World Record holder for the World's Longest Cartoon Strip. He is the author and creator of a number of comic book titles for Pocket Change Comics, including Assassinette: The Mind Stalker, Psyco Duck, Jester's Dead, The Holy Knight, Riplash, Shadow Slasher, and Warzone 3719. Bob has written two children books, Rooty the Tree Troll and Holiday Bunny; two young adult books, Mouch and Company: The Dream Psychic and Rags and Ruins; and is the co-author of Will Jones' biography A Tough Call. Bob is also the Writer/Director of the movie Dr. Prozak's Office.

TO FOLLOW BOB DIXON:
www.facebook.com/dixonbob

Made in the USA
Middletown, DE
25 October 2016